JAMAICA
A VISITOR'S GUIDE

JAMAICA
A VISITOR'S
GUIDE

Harry S. Pariser

HUNTER
PUBLISHING INC

Hunter Publishing, Inc.
300 Raritan Center Parkway
Edison NJ 08818
(201) 225 1900
FAX (201) 417 0482

ISBN 1-55650-253-2

Printed in Singapore through Palace Press

Published in the UK by:
Moorland Publishing Co., Ltd.
Moor Farm Road, Airfield Estate
Ashbourne, Derbyshire DE6 1HD
England

ISBN (UK) 086190-384-6

Photo Credits
Jamaica Tourist Board: 10, 14, 24, 34, 58, 62, 73, 113, 121, 129, 130,
137, 142, 163, 176, 193, 206, 212, 214. Roy O'Brien (JTB): 8, 109, 127.
Granville Allen (JTB): 120. Mutabaruka: 48. Jeffrey Ploskonka (courtesy of National Gallery): 56. Courtesy of National Gallery: 158. All
others by Harry S. Pariser.

CONTENTS

HELP US KEEP THIS GUIDE UP-TO-DATE

In today's world, things change so rapidly that it's impossible for one person to keep up with everything happening in any one place. This is particularly true in the Caribbean, where situations are always in flux. Travel books are like automobiles: they require fine tuning and frequent overhauls to keep in shape. Help us keep this book in shape! We require input from our readers so that we can continue to provide the best, most current information available. Please write to let us know about any inaccuracies, new information, or misleading suggestions. Although we try to make our maps as accurate as possible, errors do occur. If you have any suggestions for improvement or places that should be included, please let us know about them.

We especially appreciate letters from female travelers, visiting expatriates, local residents, and hikers and outdoor enthusiasts. We also like hearing from experts in the field as well as from local hotel owners and individuals wishing to accommodate visitors from abroad.

ACKNOWLEDGMENTS

Many thanks to my publisher Michael Hunter and his staff. For their advice and help on this edition, thanks also go to Maria Weber, Linda Rideout, Harold F. McGuire, Gail Gorthmann, Joseph Waldron, Monica Johnson, Nora Quinn, Gordon McIntyre, Diana McIntyre Pike, and Rex Nettleford.

INTRODUCTION

No other island in the Caribbean conjures up such evocative images as Jamaica. The island's name comes from the Arawak Indian name, *Xaymaca,* which means "Land of Wood and Water." Although best known for reefer and reggae, Jamaica has much more to offer: white sandy beaches framed by the turquoise ocean, the cool and misty heights of the Blue Mountains, the unique historical atmosphere of Spanish Town and Port Royal, the peaceful tranquility of Port Antonio. You'll find plenty to see and do here, a tantalizing variety of food and fruits to sample, lush and varied vegetation to enjoy, and fascinating people to meet.

THE PHYSICAL SETTING

The Land

the big picture: The islands of the Caribbean extend in a 4,500-km arc from the western tip of Cuba to the small Dutch island of Aruba. The region is sometimes extended to include the Central and S. American countries of Belize (the former colony of British Honduras), the Yucatan, Surinam, Guiana, and Guyana. The islands of Jamaica, Hispaniola, Puerto Rico, and the U. S. and British Virgin Islands, along with Cuba, the Cayman, Turk, and Caicos islands form the Greater Antilles. The name derives from early geographers, who gave the name "Antilia" to hypothetical islands thought to lie beyond the no less legendary "Atlantides." In general, the land is steep and volcanic in origin: chains of mountains run across Jamaica, Cuba, Hispaniola, and Puerto Rico, and hills rise abruptly from the sea along most of the Virgin Islands.

Jamaica: Third largest island in the Greater Antilles, Jamaica covers 11,420 sq km (4,411 sq miles). Although only about the size of Connecticut or half the size of Wales, this island encompasses a breathtaking variety of terrain. Mostly rugged and mountainous, nearly half the country is 300 m (1,000 ft.) or more above sea level. An enormous mass of limestone comprises two-thirds of the land's surface. For much of its 235-km (146-mile) length, mountains in the highlands run

Jamaica's eastern coast

across an E.-W. axis, reaching over 2,428 m (7,400 ft.) in the east. Secondary ridges and spurs gradually trail off to the narrow stretch of coast below. Jamaica was born 140 million years ago, give or take a millennium, when volcanic mountains thrust upward from the floor of the N. Caribbean. The mountains uplifted limestone formed by the accumulation of eons of dead marinelife. About 100 million years later, the mass submerged. When the East Pacific and Caribbean plates separated some 25 million years later, the stresses created major structures like the Blue Mountains and faults like the 8,120-m-deep (24,750-ft.) Cayman Trough W. of Jamaica. During this period, the East Caribbean plate slid under the North American plate, forcing the volcanic material back up to sea level. As it settled, the island shattered like a three-dimensional jigsaw puzzle. A process known as "karstification" (water dissolving limestone) produced the pits and grottos of Cockpit Country (see "Cockpit Country" under "South and West Jamaica"). This tropical weathering had the added effect of producing non-soluble mineral deposits of *terra rossa* soils. Dark red in color, they contained concentrations of aluminum hydroxide, popularly known as bauxite. This mineral, millions of years later, was to become the island's major export. The Blue Mountains, which cover the east-central area of the country, are the major range. On both sides of the island, the transition from mountains to sea is abrupt. The coastal plains are broader along the S. side than in the north. The most extensive coastal plains run along the Liguanea Plain (largely squatted by Kingston) to the plains of St. Catherine and Clarendon and on to the W. coast plains of St. Elizabeth and Westmoreland. Although there are more than 120 rivers, none is very impressive. Hector's River runs underground for five to six km of its course; the Rio Cobre forms a deep gorge at Bog Walk.

Climate

Close to ideal. The warm season is the *only* season in Jamaica. Although up to 508 cm (200 in.) of rain fall each year in parts

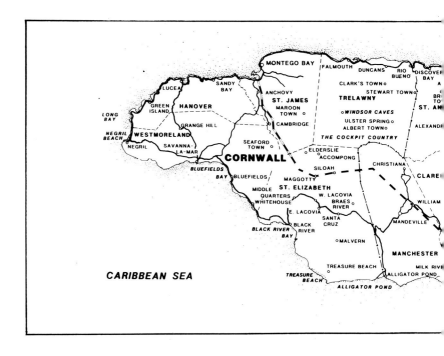

of St. Thomas and Portland parishes, the average yearly rainfall is 195 cm (77 in.), with March and Oct. being the rainiest months. Main dry period is from Jan. to March. Average temperature is 80°. Kingston averages 86.7° F high and 69.1° F low in Jan. and 90.7° F high and 75.1° F low in July. Temperatures may be 10° to 20° cooler inland. The summits of the Grand Ridge of the Blue Mountains are infrequently touched by frost during the winter months. Cloudy, cool, and damp weather may occasionally occur during the winter when "northers" arrive. Humidity tends to be high: Montego Bay may have 71–77 percent humidity; Kingston ranges from 63 percent in Feb. to 75 percent in October. But the winds really save this island. The "Doctor Breeze," a cool trade wind, prevails during the day, while the "Undertaker's Breeze" sweeps down from the mountains at night. Their combined effect is to make what would otherwise be an unbearably hot and humid environment not only tolerable but actually pleasant to live in.

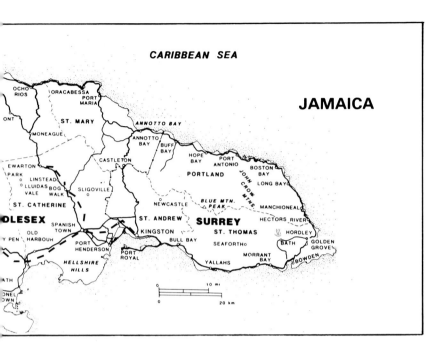

hurricanes: Cast in a starring role as the bane of the tropics, hurricanes represent the one outstanding negative in an otherwise impeccably hospitable climate. The Caribbean as a whole ranks third worldwide in the number of hurricanes per year, although they are comparatively scarce in the area around Jamaica. These low-pressure zones are serious business and should not be taken lightly. Where the majority of structures are structurally unsound, a hurricane is no joke, and property damage from them may run into the hundreds of millions of U. S. dollars. A hurricane begins as a relatively small tropical storm, known as a cyclone, when its winds reach a velocity of 62 kph (39 mph). At 118 kph (74 mph), it is upgraded to hurricane status, with winds of up to 320 kph (200 mph) and ranging in size from 100–1,600 km (60–1,000 miles) in diameter. A small hurricane releases energy equivalent to the explosions of six atomic bombs per second. Hurricanes may be compared to enormous hovering engines that use the moist air and water of the tropics as fuel, carried hither and thither

by prevailing air currents, generally eastern trade winds
which intensify as they move across warm ocean waters. When
cool, drier air infiltrates it as it heads N., the hurricane begins
to die, cut off from the life-sustaining ocean currents that have
nourished it from infancy. Routes and patterns are unpredicta-
ble. As for their frequency: "June—too soon; July—stand by;
August—it must; September—remember." So goes the old
rhyme. Unfortunately, hurricanes are not confined to July and
August. In September 1988, hurricane Gilbert devastated Jamaica. Hurricanes forming in Aug. and Sept. typically last for
two weeks while those that form in June, July, Oct., and Nov.
(many of which originate in the Caribbean and the Gulf of
Mexico), generally last only seven days. Approximately 70 percent of all hurricanes (known as Cabo Verde types) originate as
embryonic storms coming from the W. coast of Africa.

Flora

For a small island, Jamaica has a remarkable diversity of
plant life, most of which is imported from all over the world.
Originally densely covered with large trees, the island lacked
what have since become the most famous of its fruit trees,
flowering shrubs, and plants. Arriving around the 10th C.,
Arawaks brought cassava, sweet potatoes, and maize. The
Spaniards introduced bananas, coconut, sugarcane, and citrus
fruit. Still later, the British brought a number of fruits and
vegetables, flowers and trees.

trees: Over a 400-year period, Jamaica has been gradually
deforested. Once regarded as the world's finest, West Indian
mahogany was a major export during the 18th C., used in
high-quality English furniture like Chippendale and Shera-
ton. Today, however, wood is imported from Honduras because
the native Jamaican species is so hard to come by. *Mahoe,* the
national tree of Jamaica, flourishes in moist forest glades. The
rather small *lignum vitae* bears the national flower. Its name
("wood of life") refers to the medicinal qualities attributed to
the tree's resinous gum. Logwood, a native of Central Amer-

ica, is used to produce black and gray dyes. Jamaicans have long believed that *duppies* (ghosts) reside in the spreading branches of the *ceiba* or cotton tree. This enormous tree may live for 300 years or more. The aromatic native pimento tree produces a substance internationally know as allspice, because its taste is said to resemble that of cinnamon, cloves, and nutmeg combined. The useful ackee and breadfruit trees, with their edible fruits, were introduced by Captain Bligh in 1779 and 1783, respectively. Many other trees are also imports: the mango and tamarind came from India, the almond from Malaya, the casuarina from Australia, and the guango from S. America. "Macca fat" and "prickly pole" are native island palms; the royal palm is a Cuban import. The coconut palm, thought to have come from Malaya, reached Jamaica during the Spanish era. Other trees include the fiddlewood, satinwood, rosewood, West Indian cedar, ebony, Spanish elm, and the tulip tree.

others: Five hundred species of ferns, 80 species of wild pines, and at least 200 species of orchids thrive on Jamaica. Parasitic plants include several varieties of mistletoe and the dodder or "love bush." In the drier areas of S. Jamaica are numerous types of cactus, including the phallic dildo cactus and the prickly pear; several varieties of climbing cactus have night-blooming flowers. Most grasses have been introduced from abroad. Guinea and *pangola* grasses, both used for fodder, came from Africa, while molasses or Wynne grass, which has proliferated in the open areas of the Blue Mountains, was introduced by a Jamaican, Mr. Wynne. The great bamboo is a native of China. The native climbing bamboo, found in the Blue Mountains, has a 32-year life cycle. With pods reaching two to three ft. in length, the *cacoon,* a giant pea vine which grows along rivers, has been known to cover two acres.

Fauna

Like the flora, most of Jamaica's mammals have been imported. A notable exception is the coney, a large rodent which

Bamboo Avenue

superficially resembles a brown guinea pig. Once extremely abundant and considered a delicacy by the Arawak Indians, today it's found only in the Jim Crow Mountains of N.E. Jamaica. Its cousin, the rat, reached Jamaica as a stowaway aboard the earliest arriving vessels. Nineteenth C. plantation owners imported mongooses from India, hoping to eradicate the rats. At first the population declined. Then the mongooses learned to climb trees, and their culinary tastes began widening to include birds and lizards. The mongooses became so plentiful that they too became pests, and a commission was formed to exterminate them. Wild pigs roam the mountains.

Bats—known as "rat bats" locally in order to distinguish them from butterflies and moths—come in 25 varieties. Most feed on fruit or insects. With the exception of certain island politicians, vampire bats are unknown here.

birdlife: Jamaica has 25 indigenous species of birds. The doctor bird (or streamtail hummingbird), national bird of Jamaica, is found all over the island. The male's iridescent green breast and scissor-like, elongated tail make it easy to identify; the female lacks these characteristics. The name comes from its practice of puncturing the base or sides of flowers with its bill to draw out the pollen, an act which resembles the 17th C. doctor poking around with his lancet. An iridescent rainbow is revealed each time the mango hummingbird takes flight. The vervain or bee hummingbird, also found on Hispaniola, is the smallest bird on the island. The extraordinarily plumed Jamaican tody is known as the "robin redbreast." About the size and shape of a wren, it's a brilliant grass-green with a white breast; a patch of bright red feathers surrounds the throat. The rare crested quail dove or mountain witch combines bronze, cinnamon, purple, and black colors with a shaggy grey crest. The plaintive call of the solitaire can be heard high in the mountains. There are two varieties of parrots: the bright green-black and the yellow-billed. The John Crow or turkey buzzard is commonly seen hovering above. The Greater Antillean grackle (locally known as the cling cling grackle) often sneaks scraps from visitors at hotels. The grey Jamaican nightingale is identical to the mockingbird of the American South. Migratory birds include the petchary, bobolink, indigo bunting, and several varieties of warblers. Introduced birds include the Guiana parrotlet, the saffron finch or wild canary, and the cattle egret from Africa.

reptiles: Jamaican crocodiles (locally known as alligators) live on the S. coast. Anole lizards are individually equipped with throat fans of various hues. The croaker, the local version of the gecko, likes to roam up walls while holding on with its suction-cup-equipped foot pads. The Jamaican iguana, if not already extinct, is well on its way. The harmless galliwasp lizard, incorrectly identified as poisonous according to local

Turkey buzzards

folklore, lives in stony walls and rocky places. The blind worm snake burrows in the ground like an earthworm. A small boa reaches a half m in length. A constrictor which may reach a length of three m (nine ft.), the rarely seen forest-dwelling yellow snake feeds on rats and birds. The deep-throated toad, imported from the N. coast of S. America, is known locally as a bullfrog, though there are no true bullfrogs on Jamaica. There are also a dozen varieties of small frogs which are usually called whistlers or toads. Living high in the trees, the snoring frog is the second largest tree frog in the world.

insects: All told, there are more than 100 species of butterflies or "bats," many unique to the island. The largest of all swallowtail butterflies, the *Papilio homerus* has a wing span of more than 15 cm (six inches). Sought by collectors from all over the world, it dwells in the Cockpit Country and on the most inaccessible slopes of the John Crow Mountains. Jamaica is also home to the world's smallest species of butterfly: its wingspan measures less than a cm. A walking stick known as the pimento horse may reach 22–25 cm (nine–ten in.) in length. The newsbug is a brown scarab beetle which tumbles to the ground when it flies into people, considered a portent of important future events. Fireflies are so huge that they were once captured and worn as living jewels by planters' wives when attending elegant balls held on the sugar plantations. Largest among the 50 species is the click beetle known as the "peenie" or "peenie wallie." Unlike the common fireflies (known as "blinkies"), the peenie has luminous organs located just behind the head. Dragonflies (called "needlecases"), a few scorpions, trapdoor spiders, ants and termites are also common.

marinelife: The sea around Jamaica is also rich. Many of the more than 50 varieties of coral are unique to the island. Sealife includes the sea urchin, sea fan, blue marlin, and West Indian spiny lobster, and over 800 species of land shells. Green, hawksbill, loggerhead, and the rare trunk turtles inhabit coastal waters, while the pond turtle (actually a terrapin) lives in swamps and ponds. Although manatees are found off the S. coast, the West Indian seal is no longer found in Jamaican waters. Its last bastion was the Pedro Cays to the south. Whales and several varieties of porpoises are occasionally sighted off the coast.

coral reefs: Indisputably the most important living organisms in the island's history, corals produce the calcium carbonate responsible for the buildup of most of the island's offlying cays and islets as well as most of the sand on the beaches. Bearing the brunt of waves, they also conserve the shoreline. Although reefs were formed milleniums ago, they are in a constant state of flux. Seemingly solid, they actually depend upon a delicate ecological balance to survive. Deforestation, dredging, temperature change, an increase or decrease in salinity, or sewage discharge may kill them. Because temperature ranges must remain between 68° and 95°, they are only found in the tropics. Acting more like plants than animals, they survive through photosynthesis: the algae inside the coral polyps do the work while the polyps themselves secrete calcium carbonate and stick together for protection from waves and boring sponges. Reefs originate as the polyps die, forming a base for the next generation.

HISTORY

European discovery: Human history in Jamaica began when the Arawaks immigrated from the Orinoco region of the Guianas and Venezuela. The first wave arrived around A.D. 650, the second between 850 and 900. At the time of the arrival of Europeans on the island, these coastal, seagoing people numbered 100,000. Although Columbus had heard of the island of *Xaymaca* from Indians on Cuba, he "discovered" the island by accident. Sailing along the S. coast of Cuba during his second voyage, he was blown off course and caught sight of Jamaica for the first time. Later that year he set off to explore the island. Arriving on 5 May 1494, he was met by 70 canoes filled with hostile warriors. Columbus and his three caravels paid no attention to them and continued to advance, and most of the Indians fled; Columbus then used his interpreter to reassure the men in one of the canoes. He anchored at St. Ann's Bay, which he named "Santa Gloria" for the beauty of the landscape. Searching for a sheltered harbor in which to repair their ships, they found the mouth of the Rio Bueno. When Columbus ordered a boat to approach the shore, natives in a canoe came out and attacked it with blowdarts, but were repelled. When the ships anchored at the new location, hordes of curious Indians arrived; Columbus ordered his troops to open fire with crossbows, and an attack dog was set loose. The next morning, however, the Indians returned bearing bammy, fish, and fruit, and begged Columbus not to go away. After finishing his repairs and enjoying some rest and recreation, Columbus and his men sailed on 9 May to the W., where he discovered *Golfo de Buen Tiempo,* the site of present-day Montego Bay. He named the island "St. Jago" or "Santiago" after St. James.

Spanish rule: Returning nine years later, Columbus became stranded at St. Ann's Bay for one year after his two caravels sank. The first Spanish settlers, arriving in 1510, set up the small settlement of *Sevilla la Nueva* near St. Ann's Bay. Its unhealthy climate forced them to move to the place now known as Spanish Town. The Spanish enslaved the native Arawaks and, 100 years later, there were only 74 left. Succeeding them were black slaves from Africa, the first of whom arrived in 1517. The Spanish, eager for slaves to work in the gold mines of Hispaniola, decimated the native population through savage conditions and introduced diseases, to which the Indians lacked immunity. Ironically, the introduction of the first Africans as slaves was prompted by a Catholic priest, Bartolomeo de Las Casas, who was concerned about the potential extinction of the native population. He believed blacks were hardier than the Indians, and that it would be more humane to use them. Too late, de Las Casas realized his mistake. As many as three million people may have been imported from Africa over the following three and a half centuries. Many died in the bowels of the slave ships and countless others from the effects of their harsh living conditions. The Church gave its blessings ostensibly because slavery brought the heathen African under the umbrella of Christian guidance and would increase his chances for salvation. Moreover, the Spanish clergy defined the institution as one ordained by divine law. The British Society for the Propagation of the Gospel even owned slaves in the West Indies. Sugar was the oil of that era, but the Texas oilmen of their time, the plantation owners, were culturally backward to an extreme degree, and few of the fruits of European culture made their way to the Caribbean. Nothing

North coast beach

much happened to the island during the years of Spanish rule and, except for some place names, there are few reminders of their presence. For the Spaniards, Jamaica was essentially a base which supplied provisions to Spanish ships and exported lard and hides. Colonists were chiefly farmers and ranchers. A

Spanish governor ruled the island in consultation with a *ca-bildo* (council).

British takeover: Pirate ships, covertly supported by European powers envious of Spain's hold on the Caribbean, began arriving during the early 1500s, and overt raids by French and English forces continued into the mid-1600s. On 10 May 1655 a large British expeditionary force sailed into what is now Kingston Harbour and anchored near Caguaya (Passage Fort), which serves as the harbor for Spanish Town. The populace, however, had already fled to the N. coast and then on to Cuba. The angry English destroyed much of the town. Slaves, freed and armed by the retreating Spaniards, fled into the mountains and became the Maroons. In 1658 the Spanish attempted to retake the island, and their attack at Rio Nuevo on the N. coast on 27 June was the most important battle ever fought in Jamaica. Though the Spaniards were soundly defeated, the war stretched out for two more years before the island was officially ceded to the British Crown in 1660 under the Treaty of Madrid. In August 1660, troops led by colonels Raymond and Tyson mutinied at Guayanoba Vale, 15 km from Spanish Town. (Although reasons for the mutiny are unclear, it's thought to have been directed against the officious D'Olyley and continued military rule.) In 1661 the English appointed D'Olyley the first governor of Jamaica.

buccaneers and slaves: Port Royal emerged as a home base for buccaneers. Before the 1692 earthquake completely destroyed it, Port Royal had become world-renowned as the Sin City of its day. Leader of and most famous of all the buccaneers was Henry Morgan, a Welshman. Shortly after the earthquake, a Spanish fleet invaded the island. This severely damaging attack was repelled at Carlisle Bay, Clarendon. During the 18th C., Jamaica was plagued by pirates, including the legendary Blackbeard (Edwin Teach) and Calico Jack (Jack Rackham). Under the Treaty of Utrecht in 1713, Britain took over France's *Asiento* or contract for providing slaves to the Spanish W. Indies settlements. Soon, slaves were being shipped to the Spanish Caribbean in British-manned boats. In April 1782, British Admiral Rodney intercepted and defeated a combined French and Spanish fleet on its way to attack Jamaica while it was still off the coast. Near the end of the 18th C., Horatio Nelson, later to become one of Britain's greatest military commanders, visited the island. In 1739 and 1740, treaties were concluded with the Maroons which gave them some measure of regional autonomy. The sugar industry came into its own during the late 17th and early 18th centuries. Sixty-six times the size of Barbados (where the sugarcane economy had originated), Jamaica had 430 sugar estates by 1739. Of the tens of thousands of slaves imported to Jamaica during the 18th C., approximately 5,000 remained. In 1760, Tacky, a Coromantee slave, led an unsuccessful slave rebellion in the Port Maria area. Other revolts followed. The final slave uprising was led by "Daddy" Sam Sharpe, a Baptist preacher, in Montego Bay during Christmas of 1831. Although the composition of its constituency had changed dramatically, the oligarchic system of government remained intact. Its rulers were members of an elite completely out of touch with the rest of society. The Morant Bay Rebellion, led by Paul Bogle, was the culmination of all the discontent. (See "Morant Bay" under "Around The East Coast.") Although the revolt ended in failure, it led to the recall of the governor and the revamping of the constitution to Crown Colony status. The capital was moved from Spanish Town to Kingston in 1872.

the twentieth century: Jamaica was hard hit by the Great Depression of the 1930s. This depression, coupled with the devastation of the banana industry by Panama Disease, led to the outbreak of violence and rioting at Frome, Westmoreland, in 1938. Out of this chaos emerged the workings of the island's first labor unions and political parties. The Industrial Trade Union was led by Alexander Bustamante, and the socialist People's National Party (PNP) was founded by socialist lawyer Norman Manley. Labor leaders pressed for increased wages, improved working conditions, and political reform. The new Constitution of 1944 allowed for full adult suffrage. The island had become virtually self-governing; only defense and international affairs were taken care of by Britain. The tourist industry, bauxite mining, and industrialization began to flourish. The long overdue 1954 constitution transferred political power

IMPORTANT DATES IN JAMAICAN HISTORY

1494: 5 May. Christopher Columbus anchors at St. Ann's Bay.

1510: Spanish establish settlement of "Sevilla la Nueva" near St. Ann's Bay.

1517: First black slaves from Africa arrive on the island.

1658: 27 June. Battle of Rio Nuevo between the Spanish and English.

1660: Jamaica ceded to the English under the Treaty of Madrid.

1692: Port Royal destroyed by earthquake.

1760: Coromantee slave Tacky leads slave rebellion near Port Maria.

1831: Slave uprising in Montego Bay led by black preacher "Daddy" Sam Sharpe.

1865: The bloody Morant Bay Rebellion takes place.

1872: Capital moved from Spanish Town to Kingston.

1914: Marcus Garvey organizes the United Negro Improvement Association (UNIA) headquartered in Kingston.

1938: Violence and rioting erupt between workers and police during industrial strikes at Frome, Westmoreland. People's National Party founded by Norman Washington Manley.

1943: Jamaica Labour Party founded by Sir Alexander Bustamante.

1958: 3 Jan. Jamaica enters the West Indies Federation.

1960: 19 Sept. Jamaica withdraws from the West Indies Federation.

1962: 24 April. Jamaica becomes an independent dominion within the British Commonwealth.

1966: 21 April. Haile Selassie arrives on a state visit.

1981: Robert Nesta Marley dies.

1988: Hurricane Gilbert devastates the island.

from the hands of the colonial governor into those of elected representatives of the people. The PNP won the next election in Jan. 1955, and in 1958 Jamaica became a founding member of the ill-fated, 10-member West Indies Federation. Continually rent with conflicts almost from its birth, Jamaica was frequently at odds with other members. Contending that Jamaica was under-represented in the Federation which had its capital at Port of Spain, Trinidad, 1,000 miles away, Jamaica pulled out in 1961 after a referendum was held. On 6 August 1962 Jamaica became independent.

GOVERNMENT

The oldest and strongest democracy in the Caribbean, Jamaica is also the most contentious. No subject in Jamaica is so stormy, so volatile, as politics. Any visitor to Kingston will note the spray-painted slogans which denote the areas divided into "PNP zone" and "JLP zone." Politics is a passion with

Jamaicans, and polarization between the two parties makes the Republicans and the Democrats in the U.S. seem like good buddies by comparison.

political structure: After independence in 1962, Jamaica was established as a unified monarchial state. A governor general, recommended by the prime minister, represents the queen as head of state. The bicameral Parliament consists of a nominated Senate and an elected House of Representatives. Although the Senate was originally intended to be a forum of distinguished citizens which could view governmental policy with objectivity and equanimity, this has not happened. Instead, it has become a watering hole where retired politicians are sent before going to heaven or where newcomers can practice before proceeding on to the elected action down below in the lower chamber. Members of the House of Representatives—which holds the real power—are elected by Jamaicans aged 18 or older in each of the 13 parishes and the two corporate areas of Kingston and St. Andrew. The Cabinet, which is the main instrument of policy, is headed by the prime minister. Also the leader of the ruling party, he may appoint 13 of the 21 members of the Senate. The Jamaican legal system, based on English common law and practice, is administered by a Supreme Court, a Court of Appeal, and other courts.

political parties: First to evolve was the People's National Party (PNP). Founded by nationalist lawyer Norman Washington Manley, the party had its beginning in the 1938 industrial strikes. Although Manley was involved at the time in representing the industrial estate owners at the trial of the strikers, he threw himself into the task of getting his cousin, Alexander Bustamante, out of jail. He ended up settling the strike masterfully and founded the People's National Party in Sept. of that same year. Bustamante founded the Bustamante Industrial Trade Unions (BITU) in May, and put his full support behind the newly founded party. Feeling alienated from the intellectual leadership, Bustamante drifted away from the party and resigned the next year, claiming it was too radical. From 8 Sept. 1940 to 8 Feb. 1942, Bustamante was again imprisoned by the governor when he threatened to call a general strike. After his release, Bustamante lashed out at the PNP leadership and founded the Jamaican Labour Party (JLP) in 1943 in time for the first election held under the new constitution. In the Dec. 1944 elections, the JLP trounced the PNP. Although the PNP won a plurality of the popular vote in 1949, the JLP won 18 seats to the PNP's fourteen. Bustamante and the JLP swept the 1959 elections but remained the minority party in the federal Parliament because Manley's West Indies Federal Labour Party hit it big in the other islands. Neither Manley nor Bustamante held seats in Parliament, preferring to posture themselves as aloof observers. After continual challenging of Jamaica's membership in the Federation by Bustamante, Manley called for a referendum to decide the issue. On 19 Sept. 1961, the JLP won out and preparations were made for independence.

post-independence politics: In the first post-independence elections, held on 10 April 1962, the JLP made a triumphant return to power as it swept 26 of the 45 parliamentary seats. After the 80-year-old Bustamante fell ill in 1964, he was replaced by Donald Sangster who was elected in 1967 only to die in turn soon afterward. (Norman Manley retired and died in 1969, and Bustamante died in 1977.) Sangster was succeeded by trade unionist Hugh Shearer. In 1972 the reins of power passed to the PNP's new leader, charismatic Michael Manley, Norman Washington's son. Promoting himself as a modern-day Joshua, Manley flashed his "rod of correction" (received from Haile Selassie during a visit to Ethiopia) and promised to work miracles. He soon embarked on an ambitious policy of reform. In an attempt to establish what Manley termed an "egalitarian society," state control of the economy was increased, foreign ownership of agriculture and industry reduced, and grass-roots participation in the decision-making process was encouraged. New laws established a minimum wage, severance pay, and maternity leave. Rural areas were electrified, rural health clinics established, thousands of low-cost housing units were constructed, and farm land was redistributed. Manley's policies worked well at first, but they were often conceived and implemented without regard for their

wider political and economic consequences. By establishing relations with Cuba, 140 km to the N., and declaring his support
for "democratic socialism," Manley managed to alienate both
the local elite and foreign investors in one stroke. This spurred
the loss of badly needed expertise and foreign exchange with
N. America as well as a drop in U.S. aid. Reminding the
middle class that five flights a day left for Miami, Manley encouraged their exodus. The influential Chinese-Jamaican community dropped from 40,000 to 4,000 members by the end of
the decade. As conditions continued to worsen, Manley enacted a Ministry of National Security Act, resulting in the
formation of the Gun Court which had jurisdiction over all
cases involving illegal possession or use of firearms. In order
to protect witnesses, press coverage of the juryless trials was
forbidden. Until Jan. 1976, a conviction drew a sentence of
indefinite detention inside Kingston's Gun Court prison. A
National Emergency was declared by Manley in June 1976.
Although the island's economy was already in a tailspin,
Manley won the 1976 elections handsomely with a four-to-one
victory, and the situation continued to decline. Led by international reggae superstar Bob Marley, the "One Love" concert,
held in April 1978 to commemorate the 12th anniversary of
Ethiopian Emperor Haile Selassie's Jamaican visit, helped
forge a truce in the bitter political struggle, which lasted two
years.

the 1980 elections: But in Oct. 1980, accelerated deteriora-
tion in the economic and social situation forced Manley in Jan.
to call for elections—two years before his term expired. Fearing
violence or a coup d'etat, thousands left the island. Their fears
were not unjustified. In June the Jamaica Defence Force, led
by Charles Johnson, civilian leader of the small, right-wing
Jamaica United Front Party, staged an unsuccessful coup attempt. The election proved to be the bloodiest in the nation's
history. Gang warfare raged nightly in the ghettos of Kingston, and the sound of M-16 rifles and Belgian .9 mm stun guns
echoed through concrete corridors turned battleground. Land-
ing at a JLP waterfront dance site in rubber rafts, paramili-
tary troops opened fire. A dozen teenagers were cut down in
what became known as the Gold Street Masssacre. By election

day at the end of Oct., the death toll had risen to 750. During the course of the campaign, Edward Seaga accused Manley of being a Communist, and Manley countered by accusing the JLP of working with the CIA to destabilize his government. Both politicians survived the bullets fired at them, and with total voter turnout of 87 percent, 58 percent voted for Seaga and JLP.

the Seaga era: Born in Boston but raised in Jamaica, Seaga, a Harvard-trained economist who served as finance minister under Bustamante, soon set about putting Jamaica's house politically right. After kicking the Cuban ambassador off the island, he paid a courting call on newly elected American President Ronald Wilson Reagan and was received with great enthusiasm. Seaga's election caused a growth of confidence in Jamaica but, after an initial upswing, things began to deteriorate again (see "Economy"). In the fall of 1983 Seaga stunned the PNP when, in answer to one of their roll calls for a vote of confidence, he called for snap elections. Riding a popularity wave stemming from Jamaica's high profile in the farcical but popular Grenada invasion, Seaga slated elections for 15 Dec. 1983. This announcement caught Manley unprepared. Claiming that he had received a "solemn pledge" from Seaga that no elections were to be held until the new voter registration list was completed, Manley and the PNP boycotted the elections. As a result, Seaga and the JLP took over all 60 seats in Parliament.

more Michael Manley: At the beginning of 1989, Edward Seaga called for elections on February 9. Seaga had hoped to become the first three-term prime minister in the nation's history. He was running against the tide: more than 20 percent of the voters polled suggested that their reason for supporting the PNP was that it was "time for a change." Stressing the campaign theme "We are the change," Seaga attempted to neutralize his cold-fish image by having disc jockeys—with lyrics cleaned up for the occasion—play at his rallies. He described Manley's team as a "dibby dibby posse" (Jamaican for a "bunch of smart asses"). But even his promise to spend over one billion U.S. dollars on a "Social Well-Being Programme" which would have built new schools and hospitals over a five-year period, failed to sway the electorate. Indeed, in the weeks before the election, the victory-confident PNP stressed what they would *not* be able to do for their supporters. Campaigning on the dual themes of race and nationalism, the PNP's detailed proposals included inexpensive ways to improve services (such as preventive health care and nursery schools) and a promise to replace Seaga's foreign consultants with "capable Jamaicans." Capitalizing on an obscure joke made by Caucasian Seaga about monkeys, the PNP produced "This monkey can vote" buttons. While Seaga pushed for a televised debate, Manley resisted—claiming that he lacked access to the government's secrets. The election was less violent than previous campaigns. Still, there were over 50 recorded incidents of violence. In the end Manley won by a wide margin. Now in his mid-60s and having recovered from a serious illness, Manley must choose a successor well before the next election. Although party chairman and former deputy prime minister P. J. Patterson is Manley's favorite, party stalwarts are rooting for Miss Portia Simpson. Time will tell which direction the new government heads. The PNP victory was not a mandate as much as an expression of deep disaffection with the Seaga-led status quo. One thing is certain: the 1972 PNP campaign slogan of "better must come" has given way to the idea of just hanging in there.

ECONOMY

During the mid-'60s Jamaica was said to have had one of the most promising economies in the Caribbean. Yet, at the same time, it had one of the greatest disparities in income levels of any nation in the world: the upper five percent received 30 percent of the national income while the lowest 20 percent received two percent of the total. Today, that gap still exists, and it has been compounded by a US$3.5 billion debt which Jamaica can barely service, let alone repay. What has happened is that the elite of the society have attempted to live it up like their richer northern neighbors without the financial resources to do so. Jamaica has always been (and is still primarily) a plantation-style economy: exports have served to underwrite imports. In colonial Jamaica, slaves had to cultivate provision grounds, their own small plot of land, in order to help feed themselves. The surplus was sold to women called "higglers" who would resell the goods at the market. Surprisingly, along with 18th C. methods of agricultural cultivation, this system remains intact. To this day, higglers form the backbone of the internal marketing system. Higglers, however, have expanded their role and now board jets bound for Miami, Panama, and Port-au-Prince to buy goods. Returning to the island, they sell these for a substantial profit. Goods are imported in this seemingly ridiculous fashion because the government refuses to issue import licenses for them. Fundamentally a black market economy, Jamaica's most important export, ganja, is illegal (see "Ganja"). The rest of the economic sector can best be divided into bauxite, manufacturing, and tourism.

bauxite: One would never imagine that reddish rock could work economic miracles, but this ore plays a major role in the island's economy. Although bauxite had been discovered on the island as far back as 1869, it did not attract attention until the demand for aluminum increased greatly during WW II. Alcan, Reynolds, and Kaiser started production during the 1950s, and by 1957, Jamaica had become the number one bauxite producer in the world, with five million tons of ore or nearly 25 percent of the world's total. By 1975, there were five alumina refineries on the island, and Jamaica had become the world's fourth largest producer and second largest exporter of alumina. It had, however, dropped behind Australia and Guinea in terms of ore production. Jamaicans, on the other hand, were hardly making a heap of money from all of this digging up of the countryside. The original contract specified revenues of only one shilling a ton! When the contract came up for renegotiation in 1957, 11 shillings a ton was agreed upon. Yet, the government collected only US$25 million in 1973 for production of nearly 13 million tons of ore. Jamaica's leaders had discovered that, because bauxite is not labor intensive, it

Reach Falls

employs relatively few people. Although US$300 million was invested from 1950 to 1970, only about 6,000 permanent jobs had been created. Using a system known as transfer pricing, companies were undervaluing the price of the ore and reducing royalties and tax payments to a minimum. In order to rectify this situation, a bauxite levy, which indexed the price of bauxite to seven and a half percent of the price of aluminum ingot, was legislated in 1974; it multiplied revenues sixfold. Additionally, 51 percent of Kaiser's and Reynold's local mining operation were nationalized. Following this, the aluminum multinationals reduced production of bauxite and alumina and reduced imports by a third. Meanwhile, curiously enough, strikes increased fourfold. Although the levy was lowered in 1979, Jamaica had started a trend: Brazil and Australia now required that 50 percent of all mineral-based industries be owned by nationals. In 1980, bauxite accounted for nine percent of the gross domestic product (GDP). Today, bauxite production is in decline because a lack of good wars and increased Brazilian production have reduced the price for aluminum. Yet, bauxite reserves on the island are still plentiful. It's estimated that, given current output of 12 million tons per year, supplies will last for the next 150 years. Although Hurricane Gilbert wreaked little damage on the industry, US$7.5 million in income was lost during the period that plants were closed. Earnings in 1987 totalled US$336.5 million with bauxite exports increasing by 24.8 percent and alumina by 9.1 percent. Bauxite and alumina currently account for a total of 33.5 percent of merchandise exports.

manufacturing: Although most goods are imported, there is a small manufacturing sector. Since the 1950s, companies—mostly American—have been invited to establish factories, including light industries and assembly plants. However, Jamaica's 80 percent literacy rate, historically strong labor movement, and relatively high wages (compared to its neighbors) have deterred those companies seeking a fast buck. During the 1958–1968 period, the working population increased by 100,000, but only 13,000 were employed by incoming foreign firms. Unable to buy spare parts or raw materials, many factories closed. Most manufactured goods are plagued by high prices and poor quality.

tourism: After Cuba became off-limits for rich American tourists in the 1960s, Jamaica soon became one of the more popular substitutes. Between 1964 and 1974, tourism more than doubled; by 1983, 750,000 tourists visited Jamaica. Unfortunately, because tourism requires large imports of food and other materials, most locals never benefit from the tourist trade. Yet, tourism is highly productive in terms of government revenue. In 1987, about US$550 million was brought in. Although Hurricane Gilbert caused the island to fall short of its expected goal of one million visitors in 1988, tourism is expected to recover and increase in the years ahead.

economy under Michael Manley: All but the most partisan observers concede that Michael Manley's tenure (1972–1980) fell just short of being a total disaster for the economy. While some of the blame may be laid upon the intransigence of the International Monetary Fund (IMF) and skyrocketing oil prices, Manley was clearly at fault by attempting too much too soon and with too little organization to make it work effectively. Self-reliance is certainly a virtue, but it will not happen overnight. And it cannot be achieved if industries and utilities are nationalized and the elite driven away like unwanted lepers. His bauxite levy was a brilliant gamble, and without it, the economy would be much worse off today. On the other hand, he spent the revenue on public employment and welfare rather than on building up basic services and industries. By 1980, the GNP had dropped 20 percent, inflation had risen to 27 percent, the level of foreign debt had reached US$1.3 billion, and it was rumored that the economy was propped up only through sales of ganja.

economy under Seaga: Seaga's administration began with an aura of hope. At first Seaga seemed to be successful in turning the country around: inflation declined to five percent, the construction industry revived, and the tourists returned. Money poured in from the IMF and the World Bank. However, things soon took a turn for the worse. Life became more difficult for the poor as some price controls were phased out, rent control ceilings eliminated, and public housing received a lower priority. The Jamaican dollar plummeted during 1984–85, and gasoline rose 50 percent during the first month of 1984 accompanied by rises in electricity, kerosene, diesel, cooking gas, bus and air fares, and cargo rates. A further rise of 21 percent a year later for gasoline and other fuels brought three days of rioting in which ten people died.

the hurricane hits: As if the island didn't have enough economic difficulties, Hurricane Gilbert brutalized Jamaica in September 1988, killing 45 and "mashing" 20 percent of the

houses. Looting followed in Kingston and a curfew was placed
in force there until electricity was fully restored. Meanwhile,
importation of electrical generators *en masse* showed the immense financial clout of the island's black market. Gilbert was
dubbed "The Great Equalizer" because it afflicted both rich
and poor alike. In reality, the tin roofed shacks of the poor
were the first to go. And, of course, the poor are uninsured and
without the funds to rebuild. And, although Jamaica received
US$125 million in aid for the U.S. alone, many remained
openly skeptical of how much would reach those who needed
it. Aid funds were immediately the target of political in-
fighting, with the PNP exposing misuse of emergency food
supplies. In one instance, G. "Tal" Cadienhead, the JLP candidate for Kingston and Port Royal, distributed a plastic shopping bag containing food emblazoned with his image on the
outside. In another instance, Northwest Manchester's JLP
candidate Cecil Charleton received delivery of relief supplies
in government owned trucks and broadcasted on his PA system while delivering them! Food shortages were compounded
by the collapse of the silo at Jamaica's only flour mill—thus
shutting off the supply of bread and often tripling the cost of
what loaves did become available over the next several
months. Ironically, Gilbert may have helped the island's short-
term financial position because of the massive influx of aid
and the fact that Jamaica's insurance companies are re-
insured abroad. However, the cost of living rose dramatically
as many merchants tried to make good on their losses by jack-
ing up prices. Currently, CDs offer 14 percent interest and up.
But, with the *minimum* loan rate at 23 percent, inflation
seems to be built into the system. According to government
figures prices have increased overall by 820 percent since
1975. Unemployment in 1987 stood at 28 percent. While Jamaica's currency has stabilized since 1985 at J$5.50 = US$1,
its agreement with the IMF calls for further devaluation in
the case of inflation and a subsequent loss of competitiveness.
And the massive US$3.5 billion debt, whose servicing eats up
45 percent of the nation's export earnings, is a problem which
just will not go away. Unless a miracle occurs, and a massive
change takes place in the world economic order, Jamaica's future appears grim indeed.

AGRICULTURE

Nearly 60 percent of Jamaica's population lives in rural areas, but the island's agricultural economy has always been geared toward export corps rather than production for local use. While the bulk of the sugar, pimento, bananas, citrus, coffee, and cocoa are exported, rice is imported from Guyana, and corn and wheat come from N. America. Of Jamaica's 159,000 farmers, 113,000 work less than five acres each. While the average holding of large farms (500 acres or more) is 2,293 acres, the average peasant must grow what he can on 1.55 acres. A mere half percent of farm operators control 55 percent of the land, including some of the best acreage. Although the rural sector provides jobs for 37 percent of the population, it contributes only eight percent of the GNP—making it the most inefficient sector of the economy. Agricultural methods used by the Jamaican peasant have not changed in the past century. Most export crops are in decline. Jamaica had the largest banana export industry in the world until 1937, but production and demand have slacked off in recent years. The sugar industry, single largest employer in the country is in deep trouble, but Jamaica continues to produce around 200,000

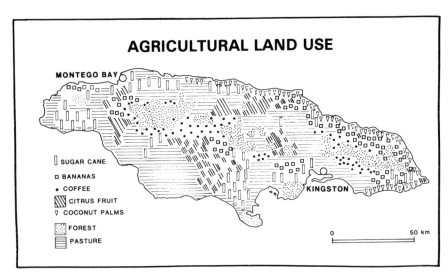

AGRICULTURAL LAND USE

MONTEGO BAY

KINGSTON

〖 SUGAR CANE

□ BANANAS

• COFFEE

〣 CITRUS FRUIT

ꛯ COCONUT PALMS

▦ FOREST

▤ PASTURE

0   50 km

tons of sugarcane. Seaga's administration stressed the production of exotic exports to North America (such as flowers and spices) while neglecting local agriculture. Jamaica continues to be a net importer of food.

post-Gilbert agriculture: Hurricane Gilbert devastated the island's agriculture, laying waste to US$49.5 million worth of bananas, coconuts, sugarcane, coffee and other corps. While sugarcane can recover in six months and banana trees in eight, it will take five years to rebuild the 60 percent of Blue Mountain coffee production destroyed, and coconut trees require seven years to bear fruit. Poultry production was also decimated. In fact the only crop relatively unaffected was the island's major cash crop: marijuana.

GANJA

Ironically, Jamaica's major export crop is one which is legally prohibited. The Indian term *ganja* is used in Jamaica to describe marijuana because that's where it originally came from. After the abolition of slavery in 1838, Jamaica's great sugar plantations needed labor; indentured servants from India began arriving in 1845. Secreting it inside their baggage, they brought the herb with them and shared it with their black co-workers in the field. Its use quickly spread all over the island. It was legal until 1913, when the jittery white ruling class, vastly outnumbered by blacks, enacted a bill outlawing the practice of *obeah* (white magic), informal back militias, and ganja smoking. Informal tolerance, however, continues to this day. The reasons for this are multifold. Although it would be relatively easy to terminate export on such a small island, the government has made only token efforts at eradication. Ganja has such widespread usage that it has become ingrained in the culture. Another reason is that it is not economically expedient to totally destroy such a lucrative source of income which provides a major income source for farmers. Although the Jamaican Defence Force on occasion blows up some of the estimated 120 or more illegal airstrips (many of which are situated on government land), approval by the government is said to reach right to the top of the bureaucratic hierarchy. It's also believed that doctors, lawyers, diplomatic corps members, and other respected, upper-crust community members are involved in trafficking. They supply the financing, while the estimated 8,000 large-scale growers provide the returns on their investment. The island's largest single cultivator and exporter is the controversial, 2,500-member Ethiopian Zion Coptic Church, a distorted offshoot of Rastafarianism, which has been indicted stateside on charges of conspiracy to import and traffic at least 15 tons of marijuana. Already the island's largest private landowner, its profits have been in invested in everything from gas stations to ricefields to coconut cookie factories. According to reports, some police are tolerant because they both use ganja and are on the take. Many police remain silent in return for a cut in cash or herb, and in some areas, they are reportedly the largest dealers. It's also a common practice for police to confiscate ganja with the intention of reselling it themselves. In December 1983, three plainclothes policemen were brutally murdered when they attempted to confiscate a ganja crop in Westmoreland Parish. Locals contended that they had no idea that the interlopers attempting to take away the product of their sweat were officers of the law.

cultivation: In some communities more than 25 percent of the households openly cultivate ganja. Cultivation for export is time-consuming, expensive, and risky. Plants must first be sprouted in a nursery before being transferred to the fields where they are continually watered, weeded, and fed with organic fertilizers. Besides taking care to avoid the prying eyes of the police, cultivators must also guard against birds and insects. Because growers rarely dare to take the time or have the necessary knowledge to cure their crop properly, the quality of even the best Jamaican marijuana compares unfavorably with top-grade Mexican, Hawaiian, and American varieties.

export: Although in the past, the government made only token efforts at eradication, the Seaga administration—acting under American pressure—did institute an eradication program. Both the Jamaican government and the DEA claim to have eradicated 65% of the crop. As a result, the State Department estimates that the amount of ganja smuggled fell to 460 metric tons in 1987 from 1,755 metric tons in 1986. Jamaica has dropped to third place among foreign suppliers of marijuana. Although Hurricane Gilbert has spurred production, ganja must now compete for space with cocaine, for which the island has become a major transshipment point.

use: Ganja is in common use in Jamaica; more than 60 percent of the lower class ingest the herb in one form or another. It may be used in tea, steeped in white rum or wine, cooked in food, or smoked. Even upper-class Jamaicans, who disdain ganja smoking as a lower-class habit, regularly ingest it as tea or tonic; it's maintained that these strengthen the blood, enabling it to stave off disease. It is also used to induce sleep, and in rural areas as a salve for infected wounds and allergic reactions. It is considered an herbal medicine rather than a drug, and Jamaican men smoke ganja rolled into five-inch paper or corn husk *spliffs*. Contrary to the popular misconception that ganja induces a state of indolent, slothful somnolence, it actually produces an energy burst sufficient for completing arduous tasks such as field work with greater speed, enabling them to work longer and harder than they would otherwise. Ganja provides a buffer against the agonizing monotony of field labor. Not only do some Rastafarians smoke an incredible amount of ganja, but it's considered vital to their religious practices; they claim it is the herb specified in the Bible. Perhaps this idea of sanctity, like ganja itself, comes from India where it's also used in Hindu rituals. In any case, Rastas swear by their weed.

finding it: Ganja is far from being difficult to obtain in Jamaica; in fact, it would be difficult to walk around anywhere in the tourist belt or even in the countryside and not be approached by someone wishing to sell it. Prices range from J$1 for a small quantity to J$20 for 50 grams or so. As with anything else, the higher the quality the higher the price. Every village or town has a ganja bar, yard, or camp where the herb, both loosely packaged and rolled into *spliffs*, is sold alongside bottles of beer and stout. *Sinsemilla (sinse* for short) is a Spanish term used to denote the highest quality weed, which is further divided into different qualities such as Lamb's Bread, Burr, and the exceedingly rare Coton. Other grades include Goat's Horn, McConey, and Collie or Kali; Bush and Mad are the lowest potency grades.

warning: One should be cautious about using ganja because legal penalties are stiff. Under the Revised Dangerous Drug Act, a first-offense conviction for possession can bring up to a J$2000 fine which may be coupled with a jail term of up to seven years. Second offenders may be fined J$5000 and imprisoned with hard labor for up to 10 years. Dealers or cultivators may receive five to 10 years in prison with hard labor. Needless to say, Jamaican jails are hardly fun places. Despite the economic importance of the drug, it is unlikely that there will be any lessening of penalties or legalization in the near future. Without the U.S. paving the way first, the Jamaican government would be unwilling to undertake such a controversial move. Additionally, damaging side-effects might occur: ganja prices might go into a tailspin, severely disrupting Jamaica's black market economy which is dependent upon regulated funds from ganja imports for financing purchases from abroad.

THE PEOPLE

Although one gets the impression from Jamaica's motto ("out of many, one people") that the country's society is composed of a number of groups living together harmoniously, such is not the case in reality. Of 2.1 million Jamaicans, 97 percent are black. Although 18 percent of these are considered to be "coloured," only three percent are of Eurasian stock and of these, only one percent are white. Thus, Jamaica is a predominantly black island with a population composed largely of the descendants of slaves, and this continues to mold the social structure. Of the Eurasian minority, influential far beyond their numbers are Indians, Chinese, and Lebanese (called "Syrians").

Beneath them in the social hierarchy is the mulatto ruling class which was created under British rule and survives intact to this day. In this stratified society, being white is often seen as being rich. (The only poor whites on the island are a group of German descent who reside in Seaford Town.) While the rich pursue their dream of "the video and the Volvo," the poor are left to just barely scuffle by. For the upwardly mobile, it is an asset to be able to document some trace of European ancestry. Jamaicans may destroy snapshots of themselves if they appear too dark in them, and newspapers have been known to flatter or malign public figures by lightening or darkening photos. This type of cultural schizophrenia is a direct result of the legacy of colonialism and reflects the fact that a secure Jamaican identity has not yet emerged. Among Jamaican blacks, skin color and physiognomy vary. This is because Jamaicans come from a variety of different tribes—Ibos, Yoruba, Mandingoes, Bakongo, Ashantis, Fantis, and Fulas—to name a few.

population: A million or more Jamaicans live in the U.S., mostly in the New York City or Miami areas; a similar number are in Britain, Canada, and other Commonwealth countries. Although the average population density for the entire island is about 477 persons per sq. mile, most habitable portions of the island have 1,000 or more persons per sq mile. More than 37 percent of all Jamaicans now dwell in urban areas, and the slums of Montego Bay and Kingston are crammed with over *2,500* people per sq mile.

male and female relationships: Jamaica's matriarchal society has its roots planted in tradition. In some African societies, matrilineal by custom or otherwise, the sexes are independent of one another. African women and their children spend their lives separate from their husbands and fathers. Wives have their own hut or room, and may own property individually. The effects of 179 years of slavery added to these customs has helped bring the present system of Jamaican social relationships into effect. During British rule between occupation and abolition (1655–1834), male slaves were allowed relationships with females only for the purposes of procreation. Prohibited from establishing long-term relationships, a

male might be sold away and never even cast eyes on the child he'd fathered. As a consequence, children were largely raised by their mothers. This system of casual alignments continues to this day. The grandmother plays a vital role in the family. The custom of the grandmother helping out came about during the days of slavery, when a mother might be sold without her children; the grandmother would then take over their care. Today, a grandmother may look after her daughter's children or even those of her son. If a daughter does not wish to be burdened with the children from a previous relationship, she may ask her mother to take care of them. After a time, she may come to retrieve them. Sometimes the mother goes out to work so that the grandmother may remain at home with the children. This type of family pattern exists not only in Jamaica, but wherever slavery has been in existence in the New World.

families: The average Jamaican lower-class couple usually lives together for a long time before they get married if, in fact, they get married at all. Contributing to this is the high cost of a wedding ceremony and reception coupled with a lack of tradition of formal marriage ceremonies. As a consequence, 40–70 percent of all births occur out of wedlock. Sex is considered to be a natural function which should not be repressed; male potency and female fertility are viewed as status symbols. A woman in her 20s who has not had a child is referred to as a "mule" (mules are sterile). Thus, over one-third of the live births in Jamaica occur among unwed teenage mothers, and the island population continues to explode. Having a child may be a way to insure a steady income, and in many cases, a woman's sole income may come from child support. In the so-called "keeper family," a man and a woman will live together. Thrown largely on his own resources, the Jamaican male has had to use a combination of his own wits and trickery to survive. The woman may go out to work against the wishes of her husband; the man will not assert his authority as the woman may break away from him at any time. Under the twin household plan, a man may set up a second household with another woman at the location where he is working.

LANGUAGE

Jamaica Talk

origins: But Jamaicans speak English don't they? Yes, but it's not quite as simple as all that. Populated by African slaves from many tribes who had to learn to speak English in order to communicate among themselves and with their overseers, Jamaica has developed its own uniquely colorful dialect. Unlike St. Lucia, where there are strong French influences in the native Creole, or Trinidad which has Spanish as well as French influences, Jamaican English has been influenced predominantly by W. African languages, notably Twi and Ashanti.

grammatical structure and language content: Both have been affected and shaped by the whims of historical circumstance. As no formal schooling was allowed under the slave system, Africans learned English in the field directly from their overseers, thus creating a unique blend of African and British grammatical structures, language content and intonation. "D," for example, is substituted for "th" as in "dat" for "that," and "de" for "the." Some aspects of intonation seem to be connected with Welsh as well, as in the dropping of the "w" sound in "woman" (pronounced "ooman") or the pronunciation of little as "likkle." Because of the immense distance from Britain, many words from Elizabethan English remain: jugs are still called goblets, small bottles are vials, and married women are referred to as Mistress instead of Missus. African influence is clear in the grammatical practice of reduplication, evident in regional dialects. A *bo-bo* is a foolish person, *bata-bata* means to beat repeatedly, and *njaka-njaka* means untidy or slovenly. More than 400 words of African origin are in use. *Duppy,* the word for ghost, derives from the Twi word *dupon,* which means the roots of a large tree. *Nyam* means "to eat," while *duckonoo* is the Gold Coast name for a dish of boiled corn. The Jamaican imagination has added many new colorful words and expressions to the English language. "Soon come" means eventually something will arrive or occur, while "walk good" is a farewell greeting. *Bangarang* is baggage; *fish-head* is a bribe, and *horse dead* and *cow fat* are irrevelant details. Jamaican speech is the product of a society stratified by more than 400 years of colonialism. Although slowly changing, the only socially acceptable speech among the Jamaican upper classes is BBC English. Middle-class Jamaicans will speak Creole only to their inferiors, consciously or unconsciously slipping back into standard English while addressing social equals.

Rasta influence: Jamaican language has been further enriched and enhanced by the introduction of Rastafarian dialect into general usage. "Irie" is now commonly used upon departing, while curse words popularized by Rastafarians, such as *bomba clot* and *rhas clot* (meaning "ass cloth"), and *pussy clot* and *blood clot* (both connoting the local equivalent of menstrual pads) are all too popular, as the rantings of any irate male will demonstrate. In Rasta talk, first person singular is always expressed as "me" and pluralized by "I-n-I." The addition of "I" in front of words (see chart) serves to increase identification with self and with Haile Selassie ("Selassie I"). If you should be asked, "Where the I live?", it means "Where do you live?"

CAPSULE RASTA TALK

Armageddon: the final battle between good and evil as predicted in the Bible.

Babylon: used to mean either the established order (Church and State), or the police or a policeman.
bandulu: criminal or bandit; hustler.
bredrin: brethren of the Rastafari cult.
bull bucka: a bully.

chalice, clutchie: the Indian chillum, a ganja pipe

dedders: meat.

Downpressor: oppressor.

dread: may mean dreadlocks, courage and fearlessness in the face of obstacles, or a dangerous or serious situation.

dreadlocks: the distinctive Rasta locks; a person wearing these locks.

dreadnut: coconut.

dunza, dunzai: money.

Elizabitch: Queen Elizabeth of England.

firstlight: tomorrow.

firstnight: last night.

fire, fiyah: Rasta greeting.

fullness: state of being full, absolute, complete

ganja: marijuana.

gates: Rasta home.

groundation: large Rasta gathering.

hail: Rasta greeting (from "Haile!" of Haile Selassie).

hard: proficient, skilled, excellent.

herb: marijuana.

I 'n' I: I; we.

irate: create.

irey, irie, iry: Rasta greeting; state of being in tune with nature, in harmony with the universe.

isire, izire: desire.

I-tal: natural foods, cooking, purity, natural style of life.

itches: matches.

ites: Rasta greeting meaning "may the receiver attain spiritual heights."

iwer: power.

Jah: Jehovah, God.

Jah-Mek-Ya, Jamdung: Jamaica.

kingman: male spouse (the king of a wife is her husband).

lion: righteous male Rasta.

lovepreciate: appreciate.

natty, natty dread: dreadlocks.

negus: king.

one love: parting expression meaning unity.

pollution: the masses of humanity living in spiritual darkness.

Rahab: the U.S.
roots: Rasta greeting; native, natural, derived from communal experience.

satta: invitation to sit; meditate, rest.
screw: to be angry.

upfull: upright.

wolf: Rasta imposter.

yood: food.

Zion: mythical Africa; Ethiopia.

RELIGION

For most Jamaicans, religion is much more than just paying lip service to vague ideals; it represents a total involvement, a way of life. One may literally eat, drink, sleep, and dream religion. As is true in poor Third World countries throughout the world, religion is very important because only religion provides respite from the constant difficulties and struggles of everyday life. For people living in acute poverty, anything which gives comfort or a hope of rising from the surrounding squalor is welcome. Major religious sects in Jamaica include the Baptist, Methodist, and Anglican churches. The United Church of Jamaica and Grand Cayman is the result of a 1965 union between the Congregational Union and the United Church of Jamaica. Other denominations include Moravians, Quakers, Roman Catholics, and a small number of Jews. Although Christianity forms the religious model for society, many African elements have crept in.

Christianity: As with culture in general, religion through-out the Caribbean is a combined affair, with an icing of Chris-tianity laid on top of the animistic rituals and beliefs imported from W. Africa. The planters—concerned more with material than spiritual benefits—saw little incentive to introduce the slaves to the wonders of the Christian God. On the other hand, depending only on fear to keep the masses of slaves in line, the masters viewed the emergence of cults with a cautious eye. Slaves could be driven to revolt by leaders who promised them immunity from bullets. Such a threat to authority had to be kept in line, and cults were rapidly suppressed. Christianity became a convenient cover for African religion, and indeed, was considered compatible by the slaves. The cults have had a longer run than the slave masters and still command consider-able influence everywhere save the Virgin Islands. Although cults like Rastafarianism bear little resemblance to African religious practices, they have deep underlying African roots.

Cults

Bedwardism: Because established religion has tended to butter its bread on the side of the government and formal reli-gious practice was actively discouraged by the slave owners, cults have always been an important outlet for religious ex-pression. One of the earliest of these was Bedwardism, which centered around the messianic folk hero Alexander Bedward (1859–1930). Born in Jamaica, Bedward emigrated in the 1880s to Panama where he had a religious vision which prompted him to return to Jamaica. In 1886 he was baptized by H. E. S. Woods, popularly known as "Shakespeare," and en-tered the Jamaica Native Baptist Church in August Town, St. Andrew. Beginning his own ministry in 1891, his fame spread far and wide. As his popularity as a healer and preacher grew, so did scrutiny and concern on the part of British authorities. Arrested for sedition in 1895 after he prophesied that blacks would crush whites, he was committed to a lunatic asylum. Released after his lawyers intervened, he remained active un-til his prediction that he would ascend to heaven on 31 Dec.

1920. Selling their homes and belongings, thousands of followers from Jamaica, Cuba, and Central America flocked to August Town. Needless to say, the expected miracle failed to occur. On 21 April 1921, he led his followers on a march to Kingston where he was re-arrested and again committed to the asylum, where he died in 1930.

black and white magic: Although Bedwardism is defunct, many other colorful cults are still in existence. *Myal, obeah,* Convince, and *Kumina* all have African roots; *myal* and *obeah,* black and white magic respectively, are the most direct manifestations of African religion in Jamaica. Now virtually extinct as distinct cults, various elements from them have been adopted by the Afro-Christian sects. The name *myal,* comes from the word *maye,* meaning sorcerer or wizard. The most important function of myalism was healing through the use of herbs and holding ceremonies at the base of *ceiba* (silk cotton) trees where *obeah* and *myal duppies* reside. While *obeah* men and women would be called upon to place spells, *myalists* would be called in order to hold ceremonies to counteract them. *Obeah* (from the Akan word *abayi,* meaning "sorceror") still enjoys a measure of underground popularity. Science, a new form of *obeah*, is based upon the magical and mystical tracts (banned in Jamaica) published by the De Laurence Company of Chicago, Illinois.

Bongo: An *obeah*-related cult is the Convince cult. Nicknamed "Bongo" and strongest in St. Thomas and Portland, it originated among the Blue Mountain Maroons. Men and spirits are seen to be co-existing within a single, unified social structure. Interacting with one another, they influence each other's behavior. Spiritual power is seen as morally neutral, and ghosts are called upon to help the living. Some are from Africa; others derive from the ancient Jamaican slaves and Maroons. At ceremonies, ghosts take possession of their devotees. Spirits enter devotees in order to further their own selfish ends; lacking a body, they long to speak, smoke, dance, and sing. Each has its own personality and idiosyncrasies. Upon possession, the face of a devotee contorts into a grimace. Ghosts may curse unrestrainedly, finger themselves through their trousers, make lewd propositions, even chase women through the yard and attempt to rape female devotees. Being possessed by a spirit has its drawbacks: hot-tempered spirits treat their borrowed bodies roughly, and may even cause physical injury or death.

***Kumina* or *Cumina*:**   Another cult that stems directly from *obeah*. Begun by Free African migrants from the Congo, its name derives from the Ki-Kongo word *kumina* (to move with rhythm). Built upon a ritual dance which accompanies exorcism, this ancestor worship cult believes that proper ceremonies must be held for the dead in order to ensure that their *duppies* will not wander about wreaking havoc. Ceremonies are held on special occasions such as rites of passage, or time of illness in the community. Services are accompanied by dancing and drumming. The larger *kimbandu* and the smaller *kyas* are the two types of drums played exclusively by males. Dancing to the drums continues until a devotee is possessed by spirits and delivers a revelation from an ancestor. The revelation may be uttered in local dialect, or in a language incomprehensible to all but those persons in trance. A goat may be sacrificed during the ceremony.

revival movements: Jamaican Revivalism started at the beginning of the 19th C. when W. African religious beliefs were merged with those of the Baptist faith to form new sects. These began to flourish during the Great Revival of 1860–61 when many Revival groups were started by established ministers. (Alexander Bedward was also shaped by this movement.) As is the case with the other sects described above, Revival sects are spirit cults; their members are possessed by guardian spirits who perform consultations and oblige favors in return for food. The two major sects are Pocomania and Revival Zion. Both share many common characteristics. Both sects have leaders (called "Shepherd" in Poco and "Captain" in Zion; female leaders are called "Mother"). Both sects hold meetings of their "bands" in a "mission ground" or "seal ground." Leaders wear turbans and are known for their ability to prognosticate. The main difference between the two sects lies in the type of spirits they worship. While Zion deals only with "heavenly" spirits (God, angels, saints, and archangels), Poco deals with "ground spirits" (the dead)— or "earth-bound spirits" (fallen angels). In general, Revival Zion, led by the flamboyant dean of Jamaican art, Kapo (Mallica Reynolds), is much less African influenced than the often disdained Pocomaniacs. Although rituals may vary between the two sects, "trumping and travailing" in the spirit is a common denominator. Deities are African gods that have been renamed Michael, Satan, Gabriel, Jesus Christ, etc. Although many of the cults described above are gradually dying out or losing ground to Rastafarianism, anyone who doubts their influence should take a stroll in or around any of Jamaica's major produce markets where cultists are frequently in evidence.

Rastafarianism

Most famous (and at times in the past, infamous) of all the sects originating in the Caribbean, Rastafarianism is also the most horrendously misunderstood. Although it has an estimated membership of just over 100,000, imposters are rife. Dreadlocks alone do not a Rastafarian make. Although their appearance may be forbidding, Rastafarians are gentle, spiritual people who really do believe in "peace and love." The name itself stems from *Ras,* the title given to Amharic royalty, combined with *Tafari,* the family name of the late Ethiopian emperor Haile Selassie; the term Rastafarian thus denotes a follower of Ras Tafari or Haile Selassie.

origins: Marcus Garvey introduced the ideas that were to become embodied in Rastafarianism. Garvey sought to unite blacks under the cry of "One God! One Aim! One Destiny!" His ultimate ambition was to return to Africa, the fatherland. In 1914 he organized the Universal Negro Improvement Association (UNIA). Headquartered in Kingston, its professed goals included a worldwide unity of the black race, the economic and social development of Africa into a model in which all black people could take pride, the development of black colleges and universities, etc. Finding he had little effect upon the middle-class Jamaicans, Garvey emigrated to the U.S. in 1916. His newspaper, *Negro World,* spread his views, capsuled as "Africa for Africans at Home and Abroad" and "Up, you mighty race, you can accomplish what you will," to 40 countries. His ideas made enemies in the European colonial and American establishment who had mineral and commodity-producing interests in the countries where he was most popular. Both integrationist blacks and communist sympathizers criticized him for not following their ideologies. In 1922 he was set up by the American government on a mail fraud charge and served two and a half years in prison in Atlanta before having his sentence commuted and being deported back to Jamaica in 1927. Garvey moved his UNIA headquarters from Jamaica to London in 1935. He died there in 1940 without ever having visited Africa. In a church in Kingston in 1927, Garvey prophesied that a black king would be crowned in Africa. In 1930 Ras Tafari, the great grandson of King Saheka Selassie, was crowned emperor of Ethiopia. Taking the name Haile Selassie ("Might of the Trinity"), he further embellished his title with epithets like King of Kings, Lord of Lords, His Imperial Majesty the Conquering Lion of the Tribe of Judah, and the Elect of God. The Ethiopian Christian Church, of which he was a devout member, considered their kings to be directly descended from King Solomon. In the midst of a severe economic depression, Jamaica in 1930 was ready for a new religion. Promoted by early leaders such as Leonard Howell, Rastafarianism soon gained currency among the rural and urban poor.

cosmology: Comparatively speaking, Rastafarianism may best be likened to a black version of messianic Judaism, or fanatical Christian sects still found in the U.S. today. The parallels are striking. Haile Selassie is the Black Messiah, and Ethiopia is the Promised Land. God is black, and Rastas are one of the lost tribes of Israel. They have been delivered into exile through the hands of the whites and are lost wandering in Babylon, this "hopeless hell," known to the world as Jamaica. The ultimate goal is repatriation to Ethiopia where they will live forever in heaven on earth. The goal of repatriation, however, has now been modified. As this is realized to be an impossible goal under prevailing circumstances, the current belief is that the status quo on Jamaica must be changed first. Ras Samuel Brown, the 1960 candidate of the Black Man's Party, was the first Rasta candidate to compete within the electoral system. Though defeated, his challenge marked a change in attitude.

Selassie's Jamaican visit and death: When Selassie arrived at Norman Manley International Airport on 21 April 1966, he was greeted by thousands of Rastas who were smoking ganja and chanting "Jah Rastafari!" Selassie immediately retreated into his plane and shut the door. Neither Selassie's lack of support for Rastafarianism, nor the military coup which deposed the Ethiopian king in 1975, failed to dampen the spirits of ardent believers. The military leaders accused Selassie of letting 100,000 peasants die during the course of the most severe drought in Ethiopia's history. (Despite Rasta theology, Haile Selassie was one of the worst tyrants in African history.) After the deposed emperor died in a small apartment inside his former palace in Addis Ababa on 27 Aug. 1975, Rastas either refused to face the facts, or portrayed Selassie as a living god who had simply moved on to another plane of existence. This follows a pattern typical of messianic cults throughout the world in which the leader lives on in the spirit after his death.

membership composition: Members are young, with over 80 percent in the 18–35 age group. Although Caucasians in general are considered to be the personification of evil, whites are considered and judged on an individual basis; many American whites have joined the sect and have been fully accepted. Women are relegated to a minor role; their only functions are housekeeping, selling crafts, etc. During the past 20 years, Rastafarianism has permeated the middle class as well as every ethnic group, but believers are still predominantly composed of the urban have-nots. Rastas are prominent among dissenters from established societal groups. The religion offers a spiritual and ideological alternative which sets its members apart from the system itself.

rituals, taboos, and symbolism: Rastas are basically vegetarians. Vegetables, fruit and juices are dietary staples. Fish
less than a foot long may be consumed, but shellfish, fish without scales, and snails are prohibited. Rastas prefer to eat *I-tal*
(natural) foods, and they avoid cooking with salt and oil. They
strongly object to cutting hair or shaving. Although Rastas are
nonsmokers and tea-totallers, their consumption of ganja is
legendary. Its many names ("wisdom weed," "wisdom food,"
"the healing of the nations") express the reverence that Rastas
feel for this plant. The very act of smoking is considered to be
a religious ritual. Like the Catholic communion cup, the pipe
Rastas use to smoke ganja is known as a chalice. Rastas usually pray to Jah Rastafari or recite variations on verses taken
from Psalms 19 and 121 before smoking "the herb." They also
cite other biblical passages which they believe sanction and
sanctify the smoking of ganja. (Not all Rastas smoke ganja,
however, nor is it necessary to smoke ganja in order to be a
Rasta.) Rastas claim they suffer no ill effects even after decades of continued daily usage. Indeed, they maintain that they
are healthy *because* they use ganja. Although not all Rastas
wear locks and not all wearers are Rastas, dreadlocks are seen
as connecting the Rasta with the Ethiopian lion; Rastas cite
biblical passages (Leviticus 19, v. 27; Leviticus 21) to support
this practice. The lion is a symbol of Rastafarianism, and as a
representation of Haile Selassie, the Conquering Lion of Judah, it may be seen everywhere. Rastas represent the spirit of
the lion in the way they carry themselves, in their looks, and
in their challenging attitudes towards contemporary social
values. Their colors—red, black, and green—are the colors of
the Garvey movement: red represents the blood of Jamaican
martyrs, black is the color of African skin, and green represents the vegetation of Jamaica as well as the hope of achiev-
ing victory over the forces of oppression. *Nyabingi* is a
Rastafarian convention, a gathering of the tribe to mellow out
together, which may last anywhere from one day to a week.
April 21, the date of Haile Selassie's visit, has become a high
holy day for the movement.

attitudes toward Christianity: Christianity is regarded
with the greatest suspicion. Even though some Rastas have

become members of the recently introduced Ethiopian Ortho-
dox Church, many have already quit out of disillusionment.
The white God of the Christians is regarded as a dangerous
deceiver because his religion denies blacks their rightful destiny (to rule the earth) and expects them to be humble while
awaiting death and the passage to an imaginary heaven. For
the Rasta, heaven is attainable here and now.

relating to Rastas: Their disturbing dreadlocks and their
consumption of marijuana can make them seem fearful. Several incidents in which Rastas shot police and soldiers have
also reinforced this false image. Despite this, Rastas are con-
genial, gentle, and trustworthy people. The *true* Rasta, that is.
Beware of "wolves in sheep's clothing," Jamaicans who seek to
exploit the popularity of Rastas and reggae by adopting Rasta
fashion without Rasta content. As a general rule of thumb, the
closer you are to tourist traps like Ocho Rios and Negril, the
greater the ratio of fakes and hustlers to genuine Bible-
thumping Rastas. Real Rastas prefer to stay out in the country
and avoid contact with the pollution of Babylon. If you want to
establish whether a Rasta is for real or not, note what he says,
what he eats, or what he smokes. If he tries to hustle you for
money, eats meat, or smokes cigarettes, chances are good that
he's not the genuine article. In general, check out the quality
of the Rastaman vibration you're receiving.

MUSIC

The roots of Jamaican music are sunk deeply in the history of
Caribbean colonialism. The ethos of musical expression in
Jamaica—indeed, in black music in the Americas as a whole—
stems from the struggle of a people wrenched out of their own
cultural milieu and thrown into unfamiliar circumstances as
well as with strangers of diverse cultural backgrounds. The
only possession the Africans could bring with them was the
space inside their heads; slave owners had no control over cultural memories. But even these memories, already dulled by
the cruel voyage overseas and the horror of slavery, were fur-

Mutabaruka

ther confused by the mingling of members from various tribes. As is so often the case in the Caribbean, a cultural synthesis emerged which forged the old into the new. What the slaves could remember, they practiced—often in the face of prohibition (playing drums, for example). What could not be remembered or only half remembered they improvised and expanded, often merging African and European elements. The music of Jamaica is an expression of the adaptation to a foreign, inhospitable environment. What is so remarkable about Jamaican music, in light of this, is its joy and vigor—in the captivating melodies of mento and calypso, in the vibrant and assertive spirit of reggae. Like American gospel, it expresses spiritual triumph in the face of hardship. Unlike gospel, blues, and jazz, which share the same roots, Jamaican music frequently includes biting social criticism and sarcastic commentary which has often been subject to the censure of authority.

Reggae

'One good thing about music, when it hits you feel okay"
—from *Trenchtown Rock*
by Bob Marley

You don't try to understand reggae; you feel it. It's not head music; it's music which hits you in the gut like a shot of raw rum. More than anything else it's a distillation of the Jamaican ethos: the sounds of the city and country, the vibrations of an island that is at once mellow and intense. Both music and lyrics reflect the realities of modern life in Jamaica. And, as such, they reflect the aspirations and struggles of Third World people everywhere.

roots: No one is quite sure exactly from where reggae music appeared. If anything, the development of reggae is linked inseparably to the maturation of the Rastafarian movement. Rasta drumming comes from Kumina drumming which, in turn, comes from Africa. The late Count Ossie and his band, the Mystical Revelation of Rastafari, were the precursors of reggae. Their songs incorporated *burra* and *funde* drumming with the sustained two-beat riff that supplies much the same trancelike effect as reggae. Reggae may be defined as the synthesis of electrified African music coupled with the influence of ska, rock steady, and American rhythm and blues. Toots Hibbert of Toots and the Maytals claims to have originated the term in his song "Do the Reggay." Certainly the Maytals were and still are one of the most important reggae groups, but their producer Clement Dodd also claims responsibility for the development of the music. Producers like Lee Perry and Island Records owner Chris Blackwell, however, have certainly had an important hand in molding the music: both helped shape the most influential band of them all, the Wailers.

history: It's impossible to evaluate contemporary Jamaican music without considering its past. Work songs were among the earliest musical developments. Part singing and call-and-response chanting were of African origin, consisting of verses led by a *bomma* with the *bobbin* (responding chorus) answering at the end of each verse. (Currently, these are kept alive only in the performances of respected Jamaican musicologist Olive Lewin and her Jamaican folk singers and in the music of the singers of the National Theater Dance Company.) Jamaica's organized musical history begins with the slave orchestras, formed by some of the wealthier planters, which would perform on slave holidays such as Picaninny Christmas and End of Crop Time. Another form, the quadrille, was the kissing cousin of the American square dance. Bands consisted of fiddle or violin supplemented with trumpet or fife. It was introduced by the planters, but slaves took the quadrille to heart and soon made it their own. Deeply influenced over the years by its American counterpart, Jamaican music flourished, producing mento, then ska and rock steady, before proliferating internationally with the development of reggae.

calypso and mento: Contrary to popularly held opinion, calypso is not indigenous to Jamaica but is an invention of Trinidad. This fallacy was fostered because calypso, having gained popularity abroad, was promoted by Jamaicans to encourage tourism. Songs like "Jamaican Farewell" and "The Banana Boat Song" ("Day-O"), popularized by Harry Belafonte, were actually written by Irving Burgie, a Brooklyn native who studied at Juilliard. Mento, on the other hand, *is* a Jamaican original. While some mento songs dealt with sad or nostalgic occasions, others were adaptations of old British folk songs or sea shanteys. Often plaintive and slow, its lyrics leaned toward the ribald rather than the political. Unlike the succinct and politically pungent content of calypso, mento dealt primarily with Caribbean sexuality in a forthright manner. Church censorship forced record sales under the counter. Instrumentation was simple: guitar, bongos and shakers, with a rhumba box—a large, wooden box straddled by the musician who plucks the four metal strips which substitute for strings. Regrettably, its 2/4 rhythm, once the mainstay of every dance or social event, has all but died out.

ska: A creation of the sound studios which invented the dance craze of the same name, ska was the early '60s Jamaican music—disorganized but cheerful and funky. Its popularity remained limited to the ghettos of Kingston and W. Indian slums of London until Millie Small's Chris Blackwell-produced hit "My Boy Lollypop" made it an international sound for a brief interim. Ska was supplanted around 1966 by rock steady, the forerunner of reggae.

the Wailers: Some give the Wailers credit for transforming reggae into its present format. Originally formed in the mid-'60s as the Wailing Rude Bwoys, the band contained Bob Marley, Junior Brathwaite, Peter Tosh, and Bunny Livingston. As they began to gain popularity in 1972, three other members were added. Despite the presence of two tightly produced, classic albums on the American market, the band became popular largely from British rock superstar Eric Clapton's cover of Bob Marley's "I Shot the Sheriff." (Needless to say, not many overseas listeners picked up on the fact that the song, dictated in Jamaican patois, was the story of a confrontation between a ganja farmer and the police.) The major label distribution and promotion of *Catch a Fire,* coupled with the American release of the Jamaican film (and accompanying sound tract), *The Harder They Come,* had a steamrolling effect on the band's popularity. No sooner had the Wailers grown popular than its members went their separate ways, with Marley changing the name to Bob Marley and Wailers. By the time of his death from brain cancer at the age of 36 in 1981, Robert Nesta Marley had become an international superstar. His influence on the music remains strong to this day. More than anyone else, he made reggae synonymous with Rastafarianism and social protest.

technique: The steady thump-thump-thump of the electric bass complements the chika-chika-chika staccato scratch of the guitar and the choppy drum sound. The resulting sound— unmistakable and instantly recognizable—resembles riding seas of rhythm with vocals supplying the melodies. Solos are not factored in, and jams are multi-instrumental funk sessions. A development that is affecting other types of music as well is the dub. Dubs originated as the flip side of singles in which the vocals had been mixed out and replaced by enhanced bass and drums along with echo techniques. The deejay and the dub poet, who talk, sing, and rap over the background music, are a direct result of the development and continued popularity of dubs.

current performing artists: Reggae has become thoroughly internationalized, and there are now reggae bands everywhere from Japan to Europe. In fact, some of the major sounds in reggae today come from Britain: Steel Pulse, the most highly acclaimed contemporary reggae band, hails from there, as do bands like Aswas and UB40 as well as the formidable dub poet, Linton Kwesi Johnson. While some musicians have emigrated, others, like Jimmy Cliff, have returned to the island after long stays abroad. Hottest rhythm section on the island is bassist Robbie Shakespeare and drummer Sly Dunbar. Dubbed the "Riddim Twins", Sly and Robbie formed an integral element in the major reggae band Black Uhuru. Roots Radics, having backed many Jamaican artists, is the Muscle Shoals rhythm section of reggae, playing on numerous studio records. They often back up poet Mutabaruka on his tours. Mutabaruka, an avowed Rastafarian who goes everywhere barefoot, was once considered to be the most likely to take up the Marley torch. Denying the title "dub poet" as limiting, Muta has gone on to use African rhythms as backing for his poems. One of the most popular reggae singers is Dennis

Brown who is backed by Lloyd Parks and We the People; Gregory Issacs, the "Cool Ruler," has been responsible for many hits. Hot island performers include Third World, Chalice, Culture, the Mighty Diamonds, Augustus Pablo, dub poet Oku Onuora, Pablo Moses, Sugar Minott, and Toots and the Maytals. Although the brutal murders of guitarist/singer/songwriter Peter Tosh and former Wailer drummer Carlton Barrett have thinned the ranks, many Marley associates and offshoots continue to produce fine music. Among these are ex-Wailer Bunny (Livingston) Wailer; the former I-Threes, Bob Marley's backup vocalists continue to make albums and solo appearances as Rita Marley, Judy Mowatt, and Marcia Griffiths.

sets and slackness: Curiously enough, as reggae rose to international popularity, its appeal diminished on the island. Today the major form of "reggae" is the dance hall style, a thumping disco-like beat centering around a deejay who sings rapid tongue twisting lyrics. It is the cousin (and perhaps progenitor) of American rap music and was pioneered by artists like U-Roy and Big Youth during the early '70s. The Marley of dancehall is the flamboyant albino Yellowman (Winston Foster) whose deejay rap songs deal with themes dear to the hearts of many Jamaicans: sinsemilla and sex. His lyrics have taken crudity, which "conscious" reggae performers term "slackness," to new heights: one of his biggest hits is called "Give Me Vagina." Second in command is Admiral Bailey who had a big hit in 1987 with "Big Belly Man." Other stars on the circuit include Ninja Man, Sanchez, Lieutenant Stitchie, General Trees, and Red Dragon. One of the worst side effects of this musical trend is that it has eliminated the need for studio musicians: deejays sing over recycled rhythms pumped out by computerized drums and bass. Likewise, the set is to dancehall what the concert is to reggae. Best described as an outdoor disco, these are mass social gatherings in which a huge bank of speakers is set up and a deejay "toasts" (introduces) songs by deejays. Everyone comes out to smoke cigarettes, drink Red Stripe beer and move and groove to the music. A new trend is to have wars between sets—two banks of speakers competing with each other in turn!

the future of the music: In the '80s reggae began to have more and more of a mass audience appeal. Many rock bands like the Police and Blondie, which incorporated reggae into their music, enjoyed a wider popularity than any native reggae band has had or is ever likely to enjoy. Ironically, much of the music has lost its social content as artists discover that they prefer Volvos to vehemence. Steel Pulse has toned down its lyrics in an attempt to secure a wider audience appeal; other acts have followed suit. Since the demise of Bob Marley the music, although continuing to mature and grow, is losing its rebel stance. While Bob Marley has been promoted to demigod status (and has become as commercialized as laundry detergent in the process), no island successor has emerged to claim the vacant throne. In fact, the major voice of social protest is British dub poet Linton Kwesi Johnson, who, ironically, has disavowed both the rigors of Rastafarian rigamarole and the title of reggae artist. (He considers himself mainly a poet.) And the major reggae artist of the decade is undoubtedly Alpha Blondy. Hailing from Senegal, he has recorded using lyrics in French, English, Mandingo, Patois, Hebrew and Arabic and has made an album with the Wailers. The inspiration for his music came during his sojurn as a student in the U.S. Although other acts like the comical Eek-A-Mouse are of value more for their entertainment than for their lyrical and musical backbones, Jamaica still seems to have deep reserves of talent. One thing is certain: reggae will continue to change, diversify, and grow as long as there are people who like to dance.

ART AND DANCE

For such a small island, Jamaica certainly is a wellspring of artistic talent. As any visitor to Kingston's National Gallery will attest, Jamaica has a large number of gifted artists who rival, if not surpass, those of any other Caribbean island, including Haiti. Moreover, it's not necessary to enter a gallery to see art. Art is everywhere, from the wall murals of Tivoli Gardens in W. Kingston to the colorful cartoons which adorn the sides of small restaurants and the carts of vendors all over the island.

artists in Jamaica: Because it was created by and for the British expatriates at the top of the heap, most early Jamaican art reflected the needs and values of the colonial power structure. Examples of this range from the pretentious marble statue of Rodney in Spanish Town—clothing him in a toga as if to claim consanguinity with the Roman Empire—to the formal oil portraits of the plantation owners. With the introduction of nationalism in this century, island art has undergone a dramatic transformation. Most visually dynamic of Jamaica's art styles, the intuitive or "primitive" art resembles that of Haiti. Jamaican works, however, are less stylized and homogenous. The movement began with such artists as John Dunkley and Henry Daley. Dunkley returned in the 1930s from his quest for fortune in C. America, and gained fame after he used his newly opened barber shop as a canvas—covering it with flowers and other patterns before taking off to put his own very special dark and prepossessing pictures on canvas. As the decades passed, the intuitive style of painting has broadened to include Rastafarianism, pastoral, and urban themes. They were followed by artists like Evarld and Sam Brown, Allan Zion Johnson, Albert Artwell, Gaston Tabois, and Sidney McLaren. One of the leaders behind this movement was the late Edna Manley, a brilliant sculptress, and the wife of Norman and mother of Michael. Other artists of note include Gloria Escoffery, Carl Abrahams, Ralph Campbell, David Pottinger, Albert Huie, and Karl Parboosingh. Far and away the most famous of them all, however, is sculptor and painter Mallica Reynolds, who paints under the pseudonym "Kapo". Leader of the Pocomania sect, he is already something of a folk hero in his lifetime. (See the remarkable special exhibition hall devoted to his work in Kingston's National Gallery.)

dance and drama: The most famous dance and drama troupe is the all-volunteer National Dance Theater Company (NDTC). Unique in the Caribbean, like saltfish and ackee they're a Jamaican specialty. Try to see one of their enjoyable performances which are held from mid-July to Mid-Aug. and in

Nov. and December. (A sampler of the NDTC's religious works is held at Kingston's Little Theater every Easter Sun. at Dawn.) Every dance form is incorporated into their material, set to background music ranging from *Kumina* drumming to Bob Marley. Another exciting and dynamic company is L'Acadco led by dancer Patsy Ricketts. The National Pantomime, now in its fourth decade, opens its season on Boxing Day (26 Dec.) each year at Kingston's Ward Theater. Its topical vignettes artfully satirize current island events. Story lines often spoof Jamaican history while taking a poke at public figures. Even if you can't unravel the patois, it's worth going to feast your eyes on the colorful sets and costumes.

FESTIVALS AND EVENTS

Sadly, many of Jamaica's traditional festivals are on the wane. Hussay or Hosay, an E. Indian festival which used to be a common sight in many towns, can now be found in only a few. And, although "Bruckins Party" is part of the dance competition in "Festival" (see below), this colorful set dance is seldom found on the once prominent holiday of Emancipation Day (1 Aug.).

Festival: Chief event on the island, Festival has broadened beyond its original intention (to celebrate Jamaica's Independence) to include a vast spectrum of events: fine arts, culinary competitions, photography, crafts, fishing regattas. From coconut-husking contests to the hoity-toity Miss Jamaica pageant, everything is included. Although Independence Day is on 6 Aug., it is traditionally celebrated on the first Mon. of the month. A parade held on that day features historical and mythical characters including Anancy, Paul Bogle and George Gordon, and Maroons and Arawaks.

***Jonkanoo* (John Canoe):** Although no one is sure what this dancing procession is exactly about, or where and how it origi-

John Dunkley, Banana Plantation

Jonkanoo

nated, the name comes from the Ewe tongue, meaning "deadly sorcerer" or "sorcerer man." Probably it originated in the secret societies of E. Africa and became linked to Christmas, the only major holiday permitted to slaves. Although Jonkanoo is recognized today as part of the island's cultural heritage, such was not always the case. In 1841 riots erupted after Kingston's mayor banned the parade. In succeeding decades it was repressed, until just a few decades ago, when it was again deemed acceptable. But with legitimization has come a corresponding decline in interest, and today, Jonkanoo dancers are no longer a common sight around Christmastime. Bands usually include a cast of colorful characters dressed in flashy rags. Featured may be a cow or horse's head, a king and veiled queen, a devil, and a few Indians. This strangely enchanting amalgam of motley characters wends its way down the road to the polyrhythmic accompaniment of drums and cane flutes.

PUBLIC HOLIDAYS

New Year's Day
Ash Wednesday
Good Friday
Easter Monday
Labour Day, May 23
Independence Day (1st Monday in August)
National Heroes Day (3rd Monday in October)
Christmas Day
Boxing Day (December 26)

EVENTS

January: Accompong Maroon Festival, Accompong, St. Elizabeth.

Chukka Cove Polo Tournament, Chukka Cove, Ocho Rios.

February: UWI Carnival, The University of the West Indies, Mona, Kingston.

Miami to Montego Bay Yacht Race, Montego Bay Yacht Club.

Red Stripe Cup Cricket Competition, Sabina Park, Kingston.

Victoria Mutual Tennis Open, JLTA Headquarters, Kingston.

The Hague Agricultural Show, Hague Agricultural Show Grounds, Trelawny.

Annual Port Antonio International Light Tackle Fishing Tournament.

The Jamaican Music Industry (JAMI) Awards, The Little Theater, Kingston.

March: Jamaica Orchid Society Show, St. Andrew High School, Kingston.

April: Montego Bay Easter Tennis and Sports Spectacular, Wyndham Rose Hall Hotel, Montego Bay.

Annual Redstripe International Polo Tournament and Horse Show.

Easter Craft Fair, Harmony Hall, Ocho Rios.

Montego Bay Yacht Club Easter Regatta.

National Dance Theater Company (NDTC) Easter Sunrise Concert.

Port Antonio Spring Marlin Tournament, Port Antonio Marina.

May: Her Excellency's May Day Charities, Kings House, Kingston.

Jamaica Horticultural Society Show, The National Arena, Kingston.

The Negril Carnival, Negril.

Manchester Horticultural Society Show, Manchester Horticultural Society Showgrounds, Ward Avenue, Mandeville.

May—June: NCB/JLTA Circuit Open/Pro Tennis Tournament, National Commercial Bank Sports Club, Kingston.

June: The Ikebana International Jamaica Show, PCI Building, New Kingston.

July: Manchester Golf Week, Manchester Golf Club, Manchester.

Annual Independence Festival events, islandwide.

August: Independence Day Festival Street Parade and Grand Gala.

All Jamaica Hardcourt Tennis Championship, Mandeville Club, Mandeville.

Two-Week Junior International Tennis Festival/Pepsi International Junior Tennis Tournament, JLTA Headquarters, Kingston and Liguanea Club, Kingston.

Reggae Sunsplash, Bob Marley Performance Centre, Montego Bay.

Push Cart Derby Finals, Kaiser Sports Club, Discovery Bay.

September: Miss Jamaica Grand Coronation Show, National Arena, Kingston.

S & P Golf Classic, Manchester Club, Mandeville.

October: Ocho Rios International Marlin Tournament.

Port Antonio International Marlin Tournament, Marina, Port Antonio.

The Pirate's Race, Port Royal.

Ocktoberfest, Jamaica/German Society Headquarters, Kingston.

October-
November: The Season of Excellence, Ward Theater, Kingston.

November: Carib Tours/Red Stripe Pro/Am Golf Tournament, Half Moon Bay Club, Montego Bay.

Annual International Show Jumping Extravaganza and Horse Trials, Cayamanas Polo Grounds, Kingston.

International Horse Trials, Green Castle Estate, near Annotto Bay.

Harmony Hall Christmas Crafts Fair, Ocho Rios.

December: Manchester Golf Club's December Party and Xmas Hamper Tournaments, Mandeville.

"Roots. Rock. Reggae," National Arena,
December- Kingston.
May: LTM Pantomime, Ward Theater, Kingston.

FOOD

No problem with eating here! Restaurants range from tourist traps and plastic fast-food joints to local dives. The latter are undoubtedly among the best places to eat. Usually the menu is written on a chalkboard inside and changes according to what is available that day. Don't let their appearance (which may be less than inviting) scare you off. Hygienic conditions are reasonably high, so there's no need to worry about getting sick. In small towns, be sure to eat early because restaurants may close early. Strict vegetarians will find a ready refuge in Rastafarian-run *I-tal* restaurants. For N. Americans or Europeans raised on a diet of fast food, Jamaica's cuisine provides a delightful change. And most dishes have a fascinating history behind them to boot, combining culinary traditions of the native Arawaks, W. Africans, British and Spanish to create new

Peppered shrimp

types of dishes which are uniquely Jamaican. The piquancy of Jamaica's cuisine dates from the period during the country's early isolation when food shipped in had to be dried, pickled, or salted. Spices were added to disguise that fact or to improve the flavor. Today, these same spices—including pimento (allspice), ginger, nutmeg, and several local varieties of pepper—give dishes their distinctiveness.

Appetizers and Snacks

appetizers: One of the most unusual appetizers is Solomon

Grundy, which is well-seasoned, pickled herring. Another is peppered shrimps. These are small crayfish caught in the streams and rivers of St. Elizabeth and Westmoreland. Boiled with salt and seasoned with local pepper, they are sold at roadside stands. Use Pickapeppa Sauce or Jamaican Hell Fire to spice up your food. Mango Chutney is one of the few remnants of Indian cuisine in Jamaica.

snacks: Roadside stands, which sell a variety of treats depending upon locality, abound along Jamaica's country roads and beaches. Patties, pastries filled with meat and vegetables, are an island staple. Stamp and Go, a name excerpted from nautical commands given to sailors in the days of yore, are fried and crispy codfish fritters. Fried fish and bammy is an adaptation of a native Arawak specialty found on the S. coast. Bammy is a fried, pancake-shaped spongy cassava bread. Once the staple food of the poor before flour became readily available, it survives today in a modified, more compact form.
Bulla is a sweet, small, but tough round cake made with flour, soda, and molasses. Fried yams, plantains, and boiled and roast corn are other common snacks. A great way to cool off and gain quick energy is to munch on a stalk of sugar cane artfully peeled for you by an island vendor. Unlike other islands, where pepperpot refers to a cassareep (cassava) stew, pepperpot here is a soup which combines calaloo greens, okra, dasheen leaves, and corned beef or pork. Jamaicans also make a great conch soup.

ackee: Most peculiarly Jamaican of all island foods, ackee and saltfish is usually eaten as a snack or as a breakfast dish. Ackee is boiled together with saltfish or salt pork and seasonings and served with dumplings (fried balls of dough) or as a sandwich. Although ackee is actually a fruit, it is always boiled before cooking in order to release the toxin (hypoglycin) inside. Because of this poison, ackee can only be picked after the pods open naturally. The pulp or aril must be thoroughly cleaned of red fiber, and cooking water must be discarded. (Ackee is rarely eaten on other islands because others are terrified of the poison.) There are two varieties of ackee: "butter" and "cheese."

desserts: Jamaica's colorfully named desserts and sweets include coconut drops, grater cake, pone pudding, Bustamante backbone, guava cheese, and matrimony. The latter is made with pulped orange and star apples mixed with cream. A feature of Jamaica's innumerable pastry shops is rock bun cookies, which are huge, chewy, and excellent. Mannish water, a tonic served at weddings or on other festive occasions, is a thick, highly seasoned soup which combines green bananas, goat offal, and any available vegetables. Duckunoo or "blue drawers" is an African sweet made of corn flour mixed with sugar and nutmeg, wrapped in a banana leaf, and steamed. The steaming imparts its characteristic dark blue coloring.

Main Dishes

Rice and peas is the standard-bearer of Jamaican cuisine. Because of its widespread popularity, it is sometimes referred to as the "Jamaican Coat of Arms." Red or gungo (Congo) peas are mixed with rice, coconut milk, and spices to form this staple dish. Curried goat, introduced by indentured servants from India, is usually served with rice and green bananas. Jerk chicken and pork is made by smoking the flesh over a pimento wood fire; Maroons, who used the method of preparation to cook wild boar, originated this legendary island specialty. The best is found on the E. coast at Boston Beach near Port Antonio. Escovitched fish is a Spanish technique in which any large fish is cut into slices and sauteed in a peppery vinegar and onion sauce. Coconut milk is boiled to a custard and mackerel, shad, or cod is added along with onions and scallions to form rundown or run-dun.

Drinks

Perhaps nothing is more important to the Jamaican than his drink. One of the most notable characteristics of the island is the plethora of shops, bars and other places serving beverages. Jamaica makes the most famous rum in the world. (In Germany, the name "Jamaica" has become synonymous with rum itself.) Distilled directly from cane in oak barrels, Jamaica's rum runs from light to dark varieties. Jamaicans, however, most commonly imbibe white rum. White overproof is the local, strong white rum. There are also a number of liqueurs, the most famous of which is Tia Maria. The most famous brand is Appleton. Jamaica's local beer is Red Stripe. The same brewers produce Dragon Stout, which competes with locally brewed versions of Guinness and McPherson. There's also a locally brewed version of Heineken (at least what the brewers *claim* to be Heineken). Beer is often drunk at room temperature or "hot." Although Jamaica is famous for its highly expensive Blue Mountain Coffee, Jamaicans, disappointingly, prefer instant. Caffeine addicts might consider bringing their own along with an electric coil. Tea, as the word is used in Jamaica, refers to any hot drink. Teas include dandelion, mint, ginger, fish, ganja, and mushroom. Be wary of the strong effects of the latter two! Fish tea is made from boiled fish broth with green bananas, other seasoning, and vegetables. Rum punch is made by combining lime juice, fruit syrup, rum, and water. ("One of sour, two of sweet, three of strong, and four of weak" runs the age-old recipe.) Wash is made with brown sugar, water, and lime or sour oranges. The prize for the healthiest drink goes to Irish Moss. Made by combining processed seaweed (agar) with condensed milk, nutmeg, and vanilla, it is believed to aid sexual prowess. A seasonal drink found around Christmas, sorrel is a cheerful, bright red drink made by stewing and sweetening the petals of flowers from the Sudanese shrub.

Fruit

In addition to commonly known fruits like mango, avocado, paw paw (papaya), pineapple, apple, bananas, guavas, and oranges, Jamaica also has a number of fruits unique to the island. Ortanique, a cross between an orange and a tangerine, was created by Charles Jackson of Manchester Parish; its name is a combination of the words "orange," "tangerine," and "unique." The crimson, pear-shaped otaheite apple was introduced along with breadfruit by Captain Bligh. Underneath its thin skin lies a sweet white flesh which surrounds the seed. Soursop is a sour, prickly fruit used to make a milky soup which has alleged aphrodisiac properties attached to it. Naseberry or sapodilla is a peach-sized brown fruit with an edible skin and delicately flavored pulp. Slightly sweet, nearly seedless, and loose skinned, the appropriately named ugli is a hybrid of a grapefruit and a tangerine. What is called cashew fruit is actually the fleshy stalk below the nut, which is eaten raw, stewed, or boiled. The native star apple is a sweet purple fruit which reveals a star shaped pattern when cut crossways. The sour pulp of the Indian tamarind tree, extracted by sucking, is a delicious treat. A hybrid between the sweet orange and the citrus plant "shaddock" from Polynesia, Jamaican grapefruit originated in the W. Indies. Really more a vegetable than a fruit, the starchy, rough and rotund breadfruit is eaten roasted, boiled, or fried. After Jamaican planters, deprived of food during the turbulent years surrounding the American Revolution, heard about the breadfruit tree, they persuaded the king of England to launch an expedition, led by Captain Bligh, to obtain it. His first attempt, on the ship *Bounty*, ended in mutiny. Although he finally succeeded in bringing the tree to the island in 1793, it was many years before it became the island staple it is today.

RECIPES

If you have cooking facilities available during your stay, you may wish to try cooking some local specialties. Here are sample recipes that should yield six portions each.

Saltfish and Ackee

1 lb. codfish
2 dozen ackees
1 large onion
1 teaspoon black pepper

3 thin slices hot pepper
1 small red sweet pepper
coconut cooking oil

After soaking codfish, place it in cold water and boil. Remove
seeds and all traces of interior red tissue from ackees. Wash
ackees three times or so. Cover and boil until moderately soft
when touched with fork. Drain, cover, and put aside. Flake
saltfish and remove all bones. Sauté thinly sliced onions and
sweet pepper rings. Remove half of the fried onions and peppers and add saltfish and the ackees, heating thoroughly and
adding black pepper. Pour on plate and add the remaining onions and pepper slices as a garnish.

Pepperpot Soup

$1^1/2$ lbs. of green vegetables (calaloo, kale, okra, etc.)
$1/2$ lb. pig's tail
$1/2$ lb. salt beef
$1/2$ lb. grated coconut
$1/2$ lb. yam
1 scallion
1 Scotch bonnet pepper
2 cups coconut water
2 qts. water

Boil vegetables with meat until tender. Purée vegetables and
return them to the pot adding coconut milk. Then add the
sliced yam and coconut. Add sliced pepper, other seasonings to
taste, and simmer for approximately one hour.

Run Down (Run Dung)

$3/4$ lb. salted shad or mackerel
$3^1/2$ cups coconut milk
1 large onion

3 medium size tomatoes
1 garlic clove
1 scallion
1 sprig of thyme
black pepper

Soak salted fish, rinse, and remove bones. Boil coconut milk until it is ready to form oil. Add seasoning to taste and simmer for 10 minutes. Add fish and cook until ready.

Rice and Peas

$1/2$ cup red or gungo peas
2 cups rice
1 pint coconut milk
salt
scallion
Scotch bonnet pepper

Boil peas in water until tender. Then add coconut milk and season to taste. Boil briskly for five minutes. Add rice and stir. Cover and simmer until ready.

SPORTS

swimming: Jamaica is famous for its beaches. Although many hotels reserve beaches for guests, access to the best is unrestricted. Montego Bay has a number, the most famous of which is Doctor's Cave. Along the North Coast, there are beaches at Damali (at Ironshore), Rose Hall, Half Moon (near Falmouth), Braco (near Rio Bueno), Discovery Bay Beach, Cardiff Hall, Alterry Beach (near Priory), Mammee Bay, Roxborough Beach, Turtle Beach (at Ocho Rios), Golden Head, and Murdocks (near Oracabessa), Pagee at Port Maria, Orange Bay, the small beaches on Peter's Island off the coast of Port Antonio, San San Beach, Boston Beach, Long Bay, Innis Bay (near Machioneal), Holland Bay (in the S. E. of the island), Prospect and Retreat and Lyssons Providence Pen (near

Morant Bay), Bailey's Beach and Flemarie (near Yallahs), Cable Hut and Brooks Pen (to the E. of Kingston), Gunboat Beach (on the way to Port Royal), Lime Cay (off the coast from Kingston), Fort Clarence and Hellshire (to the W. of Kingston), Jackson Bay, Alligator Pond, Treasure Beach, Black River, Whitehouse, Bluefields, the long stretch at Negril, and Gull Bay and Watson Taylor (on the way to Lucea).

deep-sea fishing: The best fishing is found along the North Coast and can be arranged in Montego Bay, Ocho Rios, and Port Antonio. Fish available include yellowfin tuna, wahoo, dorado, blue marlin, white marlin and sailfish.

scuba and snorkeling: An exceptionally fine place to do either. A large number of companies offer equipment rentals in all of the resort areas. If you're planning on snorkeling, it's preferable to bring your own equipment so that you will have access anytime, anywhere. Other watersports equipment is also widely available.

tennis: The Half Moon Club in Montego Bay is renowned for its facilities and instructions. There are a number of other courts including facilities provided for guests at the Hibiscus Lodge Hotel in Ocho Rios and the Admiralty Club on Peter's Island off of Port Antonio.

golf: There are a large number of courses. Tryall Golf and Beach Club (952-5110-3) is W. of Montego Bay. To the E. are Ironshore Golf & Country Club (953-2800), Half Moon Golf Club (953-2560), and Rose Hall Beach Hotel & Country Club (953-2650). Courses in the Ocho Rios-Runaway Bay area include Jamaica Jamaica (973-2436-8), Upton Golf Course & Plantation (974-2528) and Runaway Bay Country Club (973-3442-3). In Kingston try the Cayamanas Golf Club (924-1610) and the elevated Constant Spring Golf Club (924-1610). Finally, Mandeville has the Manchester Club (962-2403).

horseback riding: Chukka Cove (972-2506), Box 160, Ocho Rios, has instruction in riding, polo, and jumping available along with vacation packages. Rocky Point Stables are E. of Half Moon Club in Montego Bay. Riding is also available in Negril and Mandeville.

PRACTICALITIES

Getting There

by air: Jamaica is readily accessible from most cities in N. America. Although the only really cheap way to get to Jamaica is to swim, you can save money by sensibly shopping around. A good travel agent will call around for you to find the lowest fare; if he or she doesn't, find another agent, or try doing it yourself. If there are no representative offices in your area, check the phone book—most airlines have toll-free numbers. In these days of deregulation, fares change quicker than you can say "Jah Rastafari," so it's best to check the prices well before departure—and then again before you go to buy the ticket. The more flexible you can be about when you wish to depart and return, the easier it will be to find a bargain. Currently, most cheap fares are advance purchase with a 2–3 week limit. Departure and return dates must be set and a substantial penalty applies if you must change. For added flexibility, you might wish to purchase a "frequent flier" coupon from a dealer. This is a "free" economy class ticket which has been sold by the owner to the broker. It is then resold to you—an act which is permissible as long as you don't tell the airline. These tickets are good for one year, and the date may be changed any number of times. However, you are usually limited to class "Q" which has limited availability. Some fares are APEX (advance purchase excursion fares)—meaning you must reserve 7–21 days beforehand. Others are open, "no strings, no frills" flights, but are "capacity-controlled," meaning, buy your ticket fast! Whether dealing with a travel agent or with the airlines themselves, make sure that you let them know clearly what it is you want. Don't assume that because you live in Los Angeles, it's cheapest to fly Air Jamaica directly from there. It may be cheaper to find an ultra-saver flight to gateway cities like New York or Miami and then change planes. Fares tend to be cheaper Mon. through Thursday. Although high season is generally from around mid-Dec. to mid-April, fares also increase 1 July to 31 Aug. (around Inde-

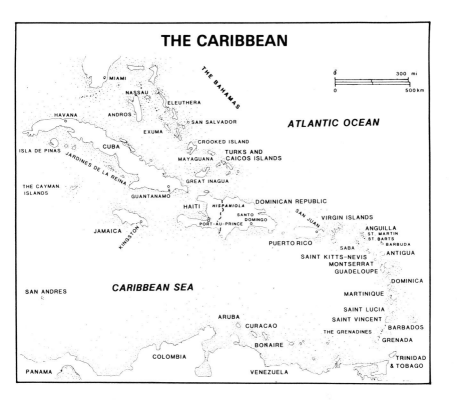

THE CARIBBEAN

MIAMI

NASSAU
ELEUTHERA
THE BAHAMAS

HAVANA
ANDROS
SAN SALVADOR

EXUMA

ISLA DE PINAS
CUBA
JARDINES DE LA REINA

CROOKED ISLAND

MAYAGUANA
TURKS AND
CAICOS ISLANDS

ATLANTIC OCEAN

THE CAYMAN
ISLANDS

GUANTANAMO

GREAT INAGUA

HAITI
HISPANIOLA
DOMINICAN REPUBLIC

JAMAICA
KINGSTON
SANTO
DOMINGO
PORT-AU-PRINCE

SAN JUAN
VIRGIN ISLANDS

PUERTO RICO
SABA

ANGUILLA
ST. MARTIN
ST. BARTS
BARBUDA
ANTIGUA

SAINT KITTS-NEVIS
MONTSERRAT
GUADELOUPE

DOMINICA

CARIBBEAN SEA

MARTINIQUE

SAN ANDRES

SAINT LUCIA
SAINT VINCENT
THE GRENADINES

BARBADOS
GRENADA

ARUBA
CURACAO

BONAIRE

COLOMBIA

PANAMA

VENEZUELA

TRINIDAD
& TOBAGO

300 mi
500 km

pendence Day) when expatriates return to visit loved ones.
The cheapest rate you can possibly hope to get is in the range
of US$210 RT (from Canada, about C$359 RT). Air Jamaica
flies direct from New York (three hours, 45 min.); Miami (one
and a half hours); Toronto (four hours); Los Angeles (five
hours); Atlanta (two hours, 45 min.); Philadelphia (four hours);
and Baltimore (three hours, 10 min.). Eastern Airlines flies
from Miami, Atlanta, and Chicago. ALM Antillean flies from
NY and Miami. Continental flies out of Newark. Northwest
flies direct from Memphis. American Airlines flies direct only
from New York City. Air Canada flies direct from Toronto and
Montreal. Jamaica may also be reached directly from anywhere in the Caribbean except Cuba and the Dominican
Republic.

package tours: As they say, all that glitters is not gold. This cliche may be old but is certainly pertinent when it comes to package tours! If you want to have everything taken care of, then package tours are the way to go. However, they do have at least two distinct disadvantages. Everything (or most things) have already been decided for you which takes much of the thrill out of traveling, and you are more likely to be put up in a large characterless hotel (where the tour operators can get quantity discounts), rather than in a small inn where you can get quality treatment. So think twice before you sign up. Also, if you should want to sign up, read the fine print and see what's *really* included and what's not. Don't be taken in by useless freebies that gloss over the lack of paid meals, for example.

by sea: With the exception of cruise ships, there's no longer any passenger service between Jamaica and other Caribbean islands. And, unless you're willing to take a cruise—which not only costs more than flying but often prevents contact with locals—no other regular transport from the continental U.S. is available. One potentially rewarding opportunity—for those who can afford it—is to sail your own yacht to Caribbean waters and travel about on your own. It's possible to crew on a boat coming over from Europe; most, however, head for the southern Caribbean so you'd have to find a way (rather expensive) up from there.

Getting Around

While not exactly the easiest island in the world to get around on, Jamaica has a reasonably efficient basic transportation network. Minibuses and shared taxis (same charge for both) run along nearly every road on the island. They are very reasonably priced, but you are unreasonably crammed. A minimum of three ride in the front and, in the case of minibuses, a total of 18 may be crammed in. Shared taxis sometimes cost J$1–2 more, but they make fewer stops because they have fewer passengers. And, as all vehicles leave only when full, they will leave relatively sooner. Although the larger buses,

particularly the new ones (Coasters), have more leg room, they also make more stops and take longer to fill up. So you must balance comfort against your schedule. In order to avoid being overcharged, ask locals the price before you leave or watch what they pay. If you give the right amount, you won't be challenged, but if you ask you may be taken for a ride. Country buses, slow and ramshackle, are frequently so packed that you often feel like a canned sardine. If you're in one, make sure you get near the window so you can get some air. Despite the inconvenience, however, they are ideal for giving you a feel for island lifestyles. All taxis sport PPV (public passenger vehicle) plates, except for "contract carriages" which have JUTA painted on them. While JUTAs have fixed fares posted, taxis are metered. Remember that night rates for taxis are higher. Drivers should be tipped. Hitchhiking is quite possible but can be slow owing to lack of traffic. If you're going anywhere off the beaten track, be prepared for a long wait. For specific travel information, see "getting there" for each area.

by rail: The sole remaining railway service in the Caribbean runs twice daily from Kingston to Montego Bay and back.

by air: Trans Jamaica flies between Montego Bay and Kingston, Negril, Ocho Rios, and Port Antonio and between Kingston and Ocho Rios and Port Antonio.

renting a car: Despite the considerable expense, the lack or inconvenience of local transportation may drive you to rent a car. Motorbikes and mopeds are also available, but a car is safer on the island's rough roads. Expect to spend at least US$50 per day plus mileage and exorbitant (US$2 per gallon) gasoline prices. Unless you have a credit card, you will be expected to leave a substantial cash deposit. You must have a valid driver's license and be at least 25 years old. Air conditioning can be a good idea—especially in the summer months. Credit cards are not accepted at gas stations, and they are generally closed by 7 PM. It may be a good idea to reserve your rental in advance. The speed limit is 30 mph in town and 50 mph on the highway. Roads are largely unmarked. Many had signs once upon a time but the environment or Jamaican drivers have done them in. In the towns signs like "one way," "do not enter," and "no parking" may be missing. Beeping your horn is not a rudeness but a mechanism for survival. Be sure to beep when you want to clear the road and can't see what's around the curve. A direction given by a Jamaican to "go straight" means to follow the main road. Don't take at face value the statement that a road is suitable for a motor vehicle because the average Jamaican doesn't own a car! Watch for deep potholes on some roads. Finally, don't forget to drive on the left.

Accommodations

Range from the very expensive to the very cheap, depending directly upon what standards you wish to maintain. With nearly a million visitors a year, there is no lack of accommodations. The problem is that most are high priced. The reasons for this include lack of a manufacturing base on the island, high interest rates (up to 39 percent) on loans, high utilities, and greed. The hotel tax and service charges can add substantially to the cost of a room. Even in the best hotels, don't expect impeccable standards and don't freak out if you see a cockroach or two. Mosquitoes will be around, save in hermetically sealed concrete boxes. This *is* the tropics after all! Avoid the all-inclusive hotels. They may seem on the surface to be a "deal" because they provide all food and cover all expenses. However, because they include all meals, they deprive you of the motivation to sample other restaurants—local and touristic. And, by prohibiting outsiders from so much as entering the grounds, they also practice a form of apartheid. Although guests are prohibited from entering rooms in many hotels, these "exclusive" resorts exclude you from the chance to meet outsiders or even have a drink with them in the hotel's bar. If you've come to Jamaica to have as little contact with Jamaicans as possible, then such a place may be perfectly suited to you. If this *is* your reason for coming to Jamaica, however, then you most likely won't be reading this book.

To make reservations from the U.S., phone the Jamaica Reservation Service (tel. 1–800–526–2422), which books higher priced accommodations listed by the Jamaica Tourist Board free of charge.

villa and apartment rentals: The Jamaica Association of Villas and Apartments (JAVA) provides home, villa, and apartment rentals. Write them at 200 Park Avenue, NY, NY or call 800–221–8830. Also try Villas and Apartments Abroad, 19 E. 49th St., NY, NY 10017, tel. 212–759–1025; and Carib Vacations Ltd., 1349 Luddington Road, East Meadow, NY 11544, tel. 516–485–0033. Airtrain International (800–268–2725) handles rentals in the Port Antonio area. In Canada, try Jamaica Villa Rentals, 10 Front Street North, Orilla, Ontario L3V4R5. Or call them at (705) 326–1616 and, in Toronto, at (416) 283–2786.

budget accommodations: The more flexible you are, the easier it will be for you to find a cheap or relatively inexpensive place. Off-season rates (1 May to mid-Dec.) are usually cheaper, but smaller places may charge the same all year long. By avoiding large hotels, not only will you save money, but you'll also have a chance to experience the country through the eyes and ears of the locals.

Larger hotels accept only US dollars, and when you add the bloodsucking hotel tax (US$4–12 per night), you end up paying through the nose. Jamaicans usually stay with relatives when they travel; if they do stay at a hotel, they often get a special reduced rate in Jamaican dollars. Still, there are plenty of accommodations for around US$10; you just have to dig for them. These places charge neither for service (usually 10 percent) or for the hotel tax. Locals will also put you up, but on an island as touristed as Jamaica, it's rarely done except for monetary gain. If you wish to stay in a small village, ask around at the local shops as to whether there are any rooms available. Remember that prices may fluctuate according to currency rates, inflation, and season. Bargaining can often save you money. One solution for travelers with limited time or for those who wish to be sure of finding a place is to hook up with Peter Bentley's Jamaica Camping and Hiking Association (JACHA). Peter has compiled a list of more than a hundred cheap places to camp or stay island-wide. For US$15, Peter will send a booklet, map, and other information detailing camping and budget accommodations on the island (write JACHA, Negril, Jamaica, or c/o Box 216, Kingston 7; tel 809–927–2097. Peter, a tour guide for SOBEK, also offers three-day Blue Mountain and other hiking tours as well as whitewater canoeing. Although you're likely to pay more if you go through JACHA, it's the cheapest alternative other than fending for yourself.

Food wagon

Other Practicalities

dining out: As mentioned earlier in the "food" section, eating out in local restaurants is an experience not to be missed. Be aware, however, that there are two types of restaurants. One serves food on plates. The other, termed "fast food," serves food in paper boxes with rice on the bottom. These are great if you want to eat in your room, are planning a picnic, or want to take off and eat when you can. But, otherwise, the former is obviously superior. Of course there are a number of American-style fast food restaurants and their Jamaican-bred imitations, like the King Burger in Kingston which is "Home of the Whamperer." Pizza is also available, but it may taste peculiar.

entertainment: If you're not in the main towns, there's not much to do at night. Much of the island's nightlife is tourist-centered and ebbs and flows with the season. However, you can have a good time just hanging out in a local bar. It's all up to you.

shopping: Retail shops are open Mon. through Sat.; in some areas shops close after noon on Wed. or Thursday. Aside from Rastafarian carved, agricultural, and woven products, there isn't much to buy in Jamaica. In fact, as most products are smuggled in from the States to avoid import restrictions, it's better to bring everything you need. Film and all photographic accessories, camping supplies, and other items are either difficult to find or prohibitively expensive. Correctly or not, Jamaicans regard their manufactured products as being inferior in quality. It might also be a good idea to bring in practical items like used clothing, batteries, etc., to trade with. Jamaican rum, acclaimed as the finest in the Caribbean, makes a nice souvenir.

food shopping: Vegetables are sold in shops, in the few supermarkets, and in the foodmarkets. Canned goods are very expensive with a can of locally manufactured coconut milk going for US$1.37 compared with 50 cents for the same item in San Francisco imported from Thailand! If cooking on your own, market shopping can be an extremely entertaining form of recreation. Smaller items, like fruit and crackers, are sold by vendors on the street from early morning until late at night. One item of interest is single cigarettes. In fact, if you've been wanting to cut down on your cigarette consumption or quit altogether, this is your chance. But the most popular items are drinking coconuts and sugar cane. The former are young coconuts which the vendor opens with a machete. He hacks off a piece from the edge which, after you're finished eating, serves to scoop out the soft white jelly inside. If you want more water than jelly or lots of jelly, just tell the vendor, and he'll hand pick for you. Sugarcane sticks are skinned and handed to you. They are then chewed and spit out. High in vitamin content, they also give quick energy.

money and measurements: The monetary unit is the Jamaican dollar, which is divided into 100 cents. Bills are 1, 2, 5, 10, 20, 50 and 100 dollars. Although US dollars may be accepted in stores and by locals (legally or illegally), the higher rate you get at the banks makes it infinitely preferable to change there. Bank rates are also highest for traveler's checks. Be careful of the Bureaux De Change, a fancy highfalutin' French name which means that you get less for your money and may incur service charges on your transactions. Hotels also offer a lower rate. The difference can be a few Red Stripes per hundred dollars. A final alternative is to change your money on the black market. But this is really advantageous only if you've got cash—which averages 10–15 percent above the bank rate; traveler's checks get about the same as at the bank. The best place to change on the black market is in the tourist shops of Montego Bay. Never change on the street. Don't change more than you need, however, because an exchange certificate is required to change money back when leaving the country. Remember, however, to have enough money on hand when you arrive at the airport to cover your duty free purchases and the J$40 airport tax.

Export or import of Jamaican currency is prohibited. Banking hours are 9–2, Mon. to Thurs.; 9–12 and 2:30–5, Fridays. Although the imperial and metric systems are in use, the country is gradually being converted to the metric system alone. Road distances are listed in kilometers. If you hear someone refering to a "chain," be aware that it's an archaic measurement which once meant 22 yards to the Brit in the street. For Jamaicans, however, it's a metaphysical concept of measurement. A "few chains" can mean a few miles.

Electricity is 110–220 volts AC 50Hz. Ask for a converter if your hotel has 220 current.

broadcasting and media: Jamaican radio and television are more or less a wasteland, offering little in the way of investigative journalism or innovative, creative programming. Jamaicans watch television programs like Dallas and Dynasty, which have absolutely nothing to do with their culture, and believe that this *is* life in the US and that this is how life *should* be lived. The evening's TV consumption serves as fodder for conversation the next day at work. Viewed as too radical by programmers, reggae is seldom heard on the radio. Many Bob Marley compositions were banned at the time of their release. Jamaican radio is most notable for the call-in talk shows which graphically illustrate the where, what, why, and how of daily life and thought processes on the island. Although Jamaica has a free press, it's monopolized by the Gleaner Company—the Rupert Murdochs of Jamaica. Founded in 1834, the *Daily Gleaner* represents the conservative business interests; as it relies heavily upon advertising, it toes the government (Labour Party) line. *The Star* is a tabloid which is the equivalent of the *New York Daily News* in terms of intellectual content. *The Record*, the only independent competitor to these two, isn't much better. Poorly printed and designed, it uses only a single page to cover news in the rest of the world.

visas: Nations of the British Commonwealth, the Republic of Ireland, and the United States may stay up to six months without a visa. Europeans may stay up to three months without a visa. With the exception of Mexico and Turkey, all others require visas. Upon arrival you must have a valid passport, an onward or return ticket and sufficient funds (this amount may be determined by the immigration officer) for your stay.

health: Hygienic standards are relatively high so illness shouldn't be a problem. Government-operated hospitals offer medical services at low rates, but be prepared for long waits. Kingston's Public Hospital is on North Street (tel. 922–0210). If you should be seriously ill, go to Mandeville which has a fairly good hospital, or better yet, Miami or New York.

telephone service: It's pretty pathetic. Pay phones are scarce and it may be difficult to find one that has not been vandalized. They can generally be found in front of the phone company and in smaller hotels and guesthouses. None of the major hotels have pay phones. Instead, you must pay $J2 per call and go through their operator. They also add a surcharge for long distance calls. On the street, there is almost always a line to get at the pay phone. Be sure to check the phone before getting into line to see if there's a coin stuck in the slot. Otherwise, you may end up waiting for twenty minutes or so for nothing. Jamaicans are usually calling long distance collect. And they use pay phones as if they belong to them. Phone may be passed from grandma to mother to "baybee" (who slurps "goo goo") back to grandma back to mother back to junior again and then back to grandma without any consciousness that others are waiting. But the same person who can keep you waiting may sweetly help you get the long distance operator—which can be quite a chore. For local calls, you must have two ten cent pieces ready. Insert them only *after* your party answers. In Kingston you will dial only the last five digits. The rules vary for other localities so ask someone before you dial. If one of the coins gets stuck, bang on the phone. For directory assistance, dial 114. To dial local intra-island long distance, dial 112. If you know the party, it's better to do it Jamaican style and dial collect. Otherwise, you should collect a stack of 30 to 70 or more ten cent coins for insertion. Begin putting in coins only after the operator tells you to do so. Needless to say, it is simpler to pay the premium and have a large hotel place the call. For international calls, you can reach the operator by dialing 113. For telegrams or international phone calls, JAMINTEL (Jamaican International Telecommunications, Ltd.) has branches in Montego Bay and Kingston. Night letters (22 word minimum) are half the price of telegrams. Local telegrams are every bit as slow as the post.

postal service: Post offices are found all over the island. Ser-

vice is slow and local letters (25 cents) may take up to a week
or more to travel from Montego Bay to Kingston. Paying for
the more expensive express service, means that your letter
will get there just as slowly but with an "express" stamp on it.
Overseas mail is cheap but equally slow. Your friends may be
reading about your trip long after you get back. No stamped
envelopes, aerogrammes, or postcards are available. Bring
your own envelopes because in Jamaica they're more expensive than the local postage rate.

information: Tourist Information Centers are located at the
airports and in Montego Bay, Ocho Rios, Port Antonio, Kingston, Mandeville, and Negril. It's best to write or call and get
information in advance before arriving. Except for the hotel
price list and Calendar of Events, the Tourist Board puts out
little in the way of practical information. The road map, available free of charge abroad, sells for US$1 in the centers. Ask
about the "Meet the People" service which will put you in
contact with locals. For background information, try one of the
branches of the Jamaica Information Service. Small parish libraries are found in main towns throughout the island. Deposits for temporary memberships are available.

theft: Petty thievery is a longstanding Jamaican tradition.
Expect this and prepare for it by exercising caution. If you are
a white (therefore assumedly rich) visitor on an island which
is 98 percent black, you'll stick out like a sore thumb. It's not
that Jamaicans are immoral; they're not. The reality is that,
given the prevailing economic situation, many must hustle or
steal to survive. Jamaicans dislike thieves as much as everyone else does. And more often than not, they themselves are
victimized by thievery. One very common crime is praedial lar-
ceny, or in plain English, crop stealing. Jamaicans have been
known to surround thieves and stone them to death. Remember, whatever you have and they don't, they want and may
steal to get. Don't flash your money or possessions around.
Never leave anything unattended—whether on the beach or
inside someone's house. If anything should be stolen, report it
to the police immediately. However, don't expect the venerable

redstripes to recover anything. They're more adept at taking bribes from ganja smugglers than at catching thieves. There's very little armed robbery compared to pilfering, so it's always better to carry valuables with you as opposed to leaving them in an insecure place. If camping, don't leave anything inside your tent that you'd mind losing.

JAMAICA TOURIST BOARD OFFICES

Jamaica

Montego Bay
Cornwall Beach
Box 67, Montego Bay
952–4425/8

Ocho Rios
Ocean Village Shopping Centre
Box 240, Ocho Rios
974–2570/2852/3

Port Antonio
City Centre Plaza
Box 151, Port Antonio
993–3051/2587

Kingston
The Tourism Centre
21 Dominica Drive
New Kingston
Box 360, Kingston 5
929–9200/19

Mandeville
21 Ward Avenue
Mandeville
962–1070

Negril
Shop No. 20
Plaza de Negril
Negril
957–4243

The United States

New York
866 Second Avenue
10th Floor
New York, NY 10017
(212) 759–5012

Miami
1320 South Dixie Highway
Suite 1100, Coral Gables
Miami, FL 33146
(305) 665–0557

Chicago
36 South Wabash Avenue
Suite 1210
Chicago, IL 60603
(312) 346–1546

Los Angeles
3440 Wilshire Boulevard
Suite 1207
Los Angeles, CA 90010
(213) 384–1123

Canada

Toronto
1 Eglinton Avenue, East
Suite 616
Toronto, Ontario M4P 3A1
(416) 482–7850

Montreal
Mezzanine Level
110 Sherbrooke Street
West Montreal, Quebec H3A 169
(514) 849–6386/7

Europe

London
63 St. James Street
London, UK SW1A 1LY
(01)493-3647
(01)499-1707/8

Frankfurt
Vogstrasse 450, 1st Floor
6000 Frankfurt/Main
West Germany
(069)597–5675

Paris
c/o Target
52, Ave. des Champs Elysees
765008, Paris, France
(1)45619058

Japan

Tokyo
Tobe Building 4-F1
2–9–17 Shiba Daimon
Minato-ku
Tokyo, Japan 105
(03)578–9012–4

CONDUCT

While traveling in Jamaica or any other Caribbean locality, keep in mind the history of the region, and the effects— deleterious or otherwise—of nearly 500 years of colonialism. Remember the injustices wreaked here and don't serve to per-petuate them. Expect to be hustled, especially on the N. coast. Don't let them get to you, and don't get angry lest you provide them with some amusement. Generally, Jamaicans are warm, gracious, and friendly people. Cultural differences are occa-sionally manifested in the language so be prepared and don't misunderstand. For example, calling somebody "white boy" is not necessarily intended as an insult but is merely a means of identification; calling somebody "fatty" isn't either as it's not considered bad to be fat in Jamaica. Never give beggars money because doing so only lessens their self-esteem and does noth-ing to better their situation. The money will soon be gone but their poverty will remain. Begging can be a kind of game or sport for Jamaicans. For example, they may first ask for $5 and then gradually lower the amount until they're only asking for a pittance. They'll keep trying as long as there's a chance of getting something out of you. Be friendly to everybody and it'll soon become evident which Jamaicans are truly friendly and which only want to get something out of you. Be fair while dealing with locals, but don't let them take advantage of you either. Deal firmly but politely with hustlers; don't let yourself be intimidated. Despite whatever problems you may have with locals, always bear in mind that the vast majority of Carib-bean citizens are decent, law-abiding, and struggling to make an honest living. As a foreigner you stick out like a ripe mango on an apple tree, so it's only natural that you will occasionally attract the more unscrupulous type of islander. There's no lack of racial tension on this island, but the level is greatly subdued compared with that of Harlem or Watts. As long as you make a civil attempt at socializing, people will accept you as a person rather than regarding you as a large strolling greenback. If you have time for the locals, they'll always have time for you. You can learn a great deal from the local society just from hanging out. If you're going only for the sun and surf, stay home and use your sun lamp and local swimming pool instead. Jamaica offers such a wealth of experience—tactile, sensual, visual, and oral—that it would be a mistake to ignore it and curl up in a concrete bungalow. Remember that, although you may be spending your vacation in what seems to you a tropical paradise, it's not a paradise for the people living there. Life has always been hard in the Caribbean, and the people have been hard-working and stoic. Don't expect conditions to be as they are in N. America or Europe. They aren't and, owing to the large population relative to the limited resources available, never will be.

women traveling alone: This can be a great experience if you do things right. It might be advisable to travel with someone until you learn the ropes of getting around. You should have no problems with men if you simply say "thanks but no thanks" when men offer you the priceless chance to spend the night with their "big bamboo." Such a response will not only cool their ardor, it may also achieve a much more desireable response. Jamaicans, like males in general, appreciate directness. So to giggle and say "maybe later" to something you have no interest in—whether it's sex or an ice cold Red Stripe—is not only ineffective but downright insulting. And you may be setting yourself up for trouble when "later" rolls around. Expect to be asked childishly imbecilic questions like "Would you like to make a baby with me?" Part of the reason for the male chauvinist attitudes prevalent here is the state of male-female relations on the island. Another is the influence of Western movies and television programs. One good way to rid yourself of trouble is to say your boyfriend is meeting you back at the hotel. If they know you are alone, they will go *everywhere* with you! Of course, if you really don't want to be hassled *period*, the best thing to do is to wear a wedding band

and carry a picture of your "husband." Traveling will be a relatively hassle-free experience as long as you exude a certain amount of confidence. And, because of the relatively strong position of the woman within Jamaican culture, the male libido is not as stifling as in Catholic or Muslim cultures. Animosity may come from young Jamaican women who resent both the apparent affluence of Caucasian women and the strong rush of desire that their men find for the white North American body. On the other hand, older women will tend to be protective of you. Women here have a great deal of pride. Don't ever make the mistake of condescending to them because they're selling and you're buying.

environmental conduct: Respect the reefs. Take nothing and remember that corals are easily broken. Exercise caution while snorkeling, scuba diving, or anchoring a boat. Dispose of plastics properly. Remember that six pack rings, plastic bags, and fishing lines can cause injury or prove fatal to sea turtles, fish, and birds, Turtles may mistake plastic bags for jellyfish or choke on fishing lines. Birds may starve to death after becoming entangled in lines, nets, and plastic rings.

photography: Film is expensive here so bring your own. Kodachrome KR 36, ASA 64, is the best all around slide film. For prints 100 or 200 ASA is preferred, while 1000 ASA is just the thing underwater. For underwater shots use a polarizing filter to cut down on glare; a flash should be used in deep water. Avoid photographs between 10 and 2 when there are harsh shadows. Photograph landscapes while keeping the sun to your rear. Set your camera a stop or a stop and a half down when photographing beaches in order to prevent overexposure from glare. A sunshade is a useful addition. Keep your camera and film out of the heat. Replace your batteries before a trip or bring a spare set. Remember not to expose your exposed film to the x-ray machines at the airport: Hand-carry them through. Finally, there may be resistance among Jamaicans to having their picture taken so use some sensitivity. Children are usually the most cooperative.

Monkey Island

What to Take

Bring only what's necessary. But be sure to bring *everything* you'll need. Even though it may be available on the island, the price may be inflated, and the item may not be available in the vicinity of where you are staying. The more extensive the travel you plan, the lighter the luggage you should carry. If you're planning on taking local transportation, bear in mind that baggage space is at a premium. A pack that converts to luggage is especially handy. Most of these are acceptable as carry-on baggage which means that your luggage won't get lost. If you check it, be sure to lock it and leave nothing of value in exterior pockets. In packing for the trip one thing to bear in mind is that there are very few laundromats in Jamaica. This means that you have two alternatives: hand washing items or having your hotel do the job for you.

basic necessities: A moneybelt, worn around your waist and under your clothes, will keep your money and documents safe. Make sure you have your passport (or proof of citizenship), driver's license or International Driving Permit, prescriptions, flashlight, batteries, and toiletries. Do not fail to bring a spare pair of eyeglasses. Glasses are prohibitively priced, and it may take up to two weeks to have them made. Likewise, any books or magazines you think you might want to read or any camping or other specialized equipment should definitely be brought with you.

useful things to bring: Scotch tape, glue, sewing kit, toilet paper, aspirin, suntan lotion, mask (plus snorkel and fins), rubber thongs, swimming trunks, hiking shorts, rain jacket or poncho, umbrella, compass.

THE NORTH COAST

Perhaps the most legendary stretch of land in the entire Caribbean, considered by many the most beautiful coastline in the
world, Jamaica's north coast is famous for its clear waters and
fine sand. Enormously rich in its variety of sealife, the long
coral reef just off the coast breaks up violent waves and keeps
all but the most determined barracuda and sharks at bay. Although a cornucopia of bleak concrete hotels has sprung up
along the peripheries of Montego Bay and Ocho Rios, much of
the coast remains unexploited. Towns like Falmouth, redolent
of past glories, are connected to chic resorts like Ocho Rios and
Montego Bay by a smooth highway which passes fragrant flowering trees with yellow blossoms, pasturelands, and rolling,
palm-covered hills.

MONTEGO BAY

Most famous of all Jamaica's tourist resorts, Montego Bay—
despite its reputation as a high-priced tourist resort town—has
much to offer the traveler. The city is divided sharply into two
sectors, touristic and residential. The latter area begins with
Sam Sharpe Square and continues down Saint James St.; its
perpendicular tributaries before Saint James St. merge with
Barnett St. and the funkier part of town. Nothing spectacular
at all here, but it's pleasant compared with the resort area
which begins just the other side of Sam Sharpe Square—here,
it's Hustler City. A burro carrying baskets filled with wilting
flowers stands under a cluster of hanging baskets; photos can
be taken for a suitable fee. Men wearing Rasta caps and a

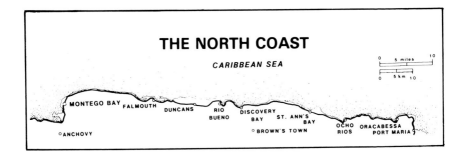

THE NORTH COAST

CARIBBEAN SEA

woman wearing a Royal Rent-A-Car ski cap sell souvenirs. This kind of thing continues all the way along the tourist treadway to Doctor's Cave and Cornwall Beach. The remainder of the concrete and glass tourist universe is scattered along the coast outside of town.

getting there: Minibuses run from all over the island to this N.W. resort town. Expect to spend the better part of a day if taking local transport from Kingston or Port Antonio. It takes several hours by bus from Ocho Rios. A train runs from Kingston via Williamsfield where you can board if coming from Mandeville. Trans Jamaica also flies from Kingston, Ocho Rios, Port Antonio, and Negril.

arriving by air: After your plane touches down on the runway, you may notice your stewardess running amuck with a spray can. It contains an insecticide, and its use is dictated by WHO regulations. As long as you have your identification and your return or onward ticket, immigrations and customs should be speedy. Before the immigrations counter is the tourist information and rum courtesy booth. Sip your rum drink and see if tourist information has any information available (sometimes they are out). If you're taking a taxi to your hotel, ask them for the correct rate. The foreign exchange booths lie just past immigration to the rear. Theoretically, they should be in attendance to meet all flights. But they are often closed late at night. So, if you're going to be arriving late, you would be well advised to import some currency "illegally" to tide you over. The baggage claim area is downstairs. If your luggage has been sent by Eastern to Bogota or wherever, you will be

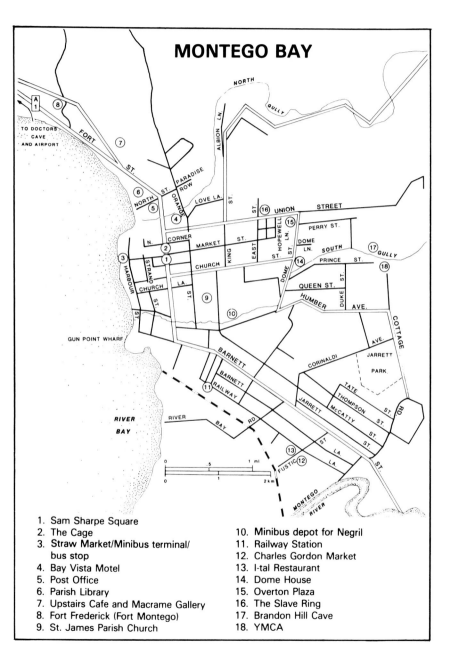

MONTEGO BAY

NORTH

GULLY

TO DOCTORS CAVE AND AIRPORT

A 1

FORT ST.

ST.

PARADISE ROW

ALBION LN.

NORTH

ORANGE ST.

LOVE LA.

ST.

UNION STREET

CORNER

MARKET ST.

KING ST.

EAST ST.

HOPEWELL LN.

PERRY ST.

DOME LN.

DOME ST.

SOUTH GULLY

CHURCH ST.

HARBOUR ST.

STRAND ST.

CHURCH ST.

CHURCH LA.

ST.

PRINCE ST.

QUEEN ST.

DUKE ST.

HUMBER AVE.

COTTAGE

GUN POINT WHARF

BARNETT

BARNETT RAILWAY

CORINALDI

JARRETT PARK

AVE.

TATE ST.

THOMPSON ST.

RIVER BAY

RIVER

BAY RD.

JARRETT

McCATTY ST.

ST.

RD.

ST.

LA.

0 .5 1 mi
0 1 2 km

FUSTIC LA.

MONTEGO RIVER

1. Sam Sharpe Square
2. The Cage
3. Straw Market/Minibus terminal/ bus stop
4. Bay Vista Motel
5. Post Office
6. Parish Library
7. Upstairs Cafe and Macrame Gallery
8. Fort Frederick (Fort Montego)
9. St. James Parish Church

10. Minibus depot for Negril
11. Railway Station
12. Charles Gordon Market
13. I-tal Restaurant
14. Dome House
15. Overton Plaza
16. The Slave Ring
17. Brandon Hill Cave
18. YMCA

required to fill out a form and return to the airport to pick up
your luggage. Outside, you will meet one of the worst aspects
of Jamaica face-to-face: hustling rip-off taxi drivers. If you
don't have much luggage, you have two other options. You can
walk to your hotel if it's reasonably close. Or you can walk up
to the roundabout, walk down to the bus stand on the right,
and take a bus, minibus, or shared taxi to town. This should
run you from J$1–2.

history: When Columbus was cruising the Caribbean and
discovering things, he anchored at the port now known as
Montego Bay. Here, an Arawak volunteer joined his crew.
Upon departure, the wind blew toward Cuba so Columbus, ac-
cordingly, named Montego Bay *El Golfo de Buen Tiempo* (Fair
Weather Gulf). It was not until 1655 that Montego Bay was
noted on Spanish maps as *Manterias*. The name Montego derives from *manteca*, the Spanish word for butter or lard—
Spanish settlers once used the bay to ship pig and cattle fat,
popularly known as hog's butter. The Parish of St. James was
formed by the British in 1665. A 1711 description related that
it had no towns, little commerce, and few inhabitants. Because
the presence of Maroons and pirates deterred settlers, Montego Bay didn't really take off as a settlement until the last
half of the 18th century. During the winter of 1831–32 the
town was involved in Jamaica's most serious slave rebellion. It
began at Kensington Estate, a few miles inland, and ended
with a million pounds in property damage, along with the
courtmartial and execution of Sam Sharpe and 500 of his followers. A member of the anti-slavery Baptists, Sharpe planned
a three-day sit-down strike to take place just after Christmas.
Ironically, his plans were circumvented when some of his followers broke into a rum store on the estate and, after getting
plastered, set fire to buildings and cane fields. Serving as a
signal for slaves on other estates, the red glow of flames spread
to nearby hills. Although Sharpe was executed, his revolt
forced a reconsideration of slavery, and the British Parliament
moved to abolish the practice throughout the British Empire
in 1834.

sights: Truthfully, there's not a great deal to see in Montego
Bay. The main thing to do is walk through the street and savor

the atmosphere. While you're at it, you might consider stopping in at a few places. More noteworthy for its history than its appearance is Fort Frederick, which overlooks the inner harbor area. In 1760, a gunner, setting off a volley in celebration of the surrender of Havana, had a cannon blow up in his face. In 1795, the fort fired several volleys at the English schooner *Mercury*, mistaking it for a French privateer. Presently, the place is used as a lover's lane at night: great place to bring your girlfriend or boyfriend. The Cage, the stone structure in Sam Sharpe Square, was used to confine runaway slaves, disorderly drunks, and other vagrants. Since then it's been used as a latrine for government employees, a TB clinic, travel agency, and as a tour booking office. The refurbished square holds five bronze statues which stand in front of The Cage. The work of Jamaican sculptress Kay Sullivan, they portray Sam, bible in hand, preaching to the other four. Political meetings are held in the square, and announcements of new elections and candidacies have been made here.

At the corner of Creek and Dome streets, the Dome, once the only reliable source of water, and now in a state of abject disrepair, was built in 1837. An official called the "Keeper of the Keys" lived, for many years, on the upper floor. Saint James Parish Church, constructed during 1775–82, was damaged by the very severe tremors of the 1957 earthquake and then rebuilt. A relic from an era of bygone affluence, its gardenlike churchyard contains the ostentatious funeral monuments of Jamaican planters—well worth a visit. Resting under the shade of a silk cotton tree, the Slave Ring, located at the corner of East and Union streets, was first used as a slave market and later as a pit for fighting cocks. Brandon Hill Cave, reached by a path located behind the houses at the end of Princess St., has a 25-m-deep rock chamber. The United Fruit Company Wharf, reached by Fish Lane from Barnett St., is the larger of the two banana wharves. See the flurry of activity which accompanies the arrival and departure of a banana boat. The address 12^1/$_2$ King St. is the location of Canterbury, a sprawling squatter settlement in which more than 2,000 humble abodes are crammed onto only a few acres. Quite a contrast to the homes of the ultra-rich set high on the hills above.

Formerly the Bogue Islands, the Montego Freeport was created through a combination of dumping and dredging in the 1960s. It now contains Seawind Beach Resort, the Bob Marley Performing Centre, the Montego Bay Yacht club, and docks and a shopping center for cruise ships.

beaches: The only free beach in Montego Bay is a small stretch of sand situated next to Walter Fletcher Beach. Walter Fletcher Beach is now the site of a complex including tennis, netball, and volleyball courts, changing rooms, restaurant, and souvenir shops (open daily 8:30–5, J$3 admission). Farther up the strip is Doctor's Cave Beach, the most famous beach in all Jamaica. Originally an isolated spot with nothing nearby except tombstones, it was developed and then donated to the town by Dr. Alexander McCatty in 1906. The town rented the beach to a club, and as a result of pressure from the club, in 1929 the town agreed to rent the adjacent Silver Sands Beach. (It was feared that foreign visitors would be driven away if the beach were open to all.) Doctor's Cave was destroyed by the 1932 hurricane, and today, what you see is all you get. There's excellent snorkeling on the reef; hire a glass-bottomed boat (J$25 or negotiate for less) for an hour. (The boat is of less use to get you to the reef than to protect you from the jet skis, power boats and yachts that cruise back and forth.) Open daily 8:30–5, J$4 admission includes the use of a locker for valuables. The "supermarket" on the second floor at Ricky's (across from the beach) has fresh juices and lower liquor prices than markets in town. Cornwall Beach, across from Casa Montego, is the smallest of all (open daily 9–5, J$2 admission).

accommodations: There is a tremendous variety of hotels to choose among, and hotels are located in a number of different areas. The three luxury hotels are well out of town. While Half Moon Club lies to the east, Round Hill and Tryall are to the west. Kent Avenue, behind the airport, has Sandals and Holiday House. Other hotels are on the way to Rose Hall and Falmouth. A large number are grouped between the airport and Sam Sharpe Square. Town itself has a few. And Seawind Beach Resort lies to the south. One of the most centrally located of all hotels is the attractive Doctor's Cave Beach Hotel. It lies across from the entrance to Doctor's Cave Beach. It has 85 comfortable a/c rooms and a variety of plans (EP, CP, MAP) available. There's a pool located next to the outdoor bar. The photos on the wall are the work of Andre McGann, son of the owner. The artwork is by former manager Ned Wong. See the chart for rates.

budget accommodations: Down the road from the airport lies Ocean View Guest House which offers the best rates of any hotel recommended by the tourist board. If you're arriving at night or planning to leave on an early flight, this is the place to stay. It's run by outgoing and friendly Wayne Matthews, his American wife Donna, and their mother. There's a central dining room with a TV which leads to a balcony with chaise lounges. Meals are available upon request. Rooms are a/c and each has private bath. If Ocean View is full, higher priced Seville is just a bit farther down the road. See chart for rates. The best bet out of town is Damali Beach Village (tel. 953–2387) which has both rooms and camping sites. Located in town at 28 Humbler Avenue, the YMCA (tel. 952–5368) is safe, secure, and reasonably priced at around US$10 s or $14 d. Special group rates for the 15 rooms are available, and rates are the same all year round save Sunsplash time when this famous music festival draws crowds. Shared bathrooms (biblically labeled "John" and "Mary") are down the hall, a lounge room has a TV, and there are table tennis tables downstairs. Less desirable places to stay and equally expensive are the local bars in town (like Lyle's Intensified) and the centrally located Bay Vista Motel. If you're intent on staying on for some days, you may wish to inquire about renting a room from locals.

dining out: Prices go up with cleanliness and atmosphere. If you're staying out along the tourist strip, it's a long walk to town. There are too many tourist-oriented restaurants to sample during one stay. One of the best known is the Coconut

MONTEGO BAY ACCOMMODATIONS

KEY: S = Single; D = Double; 3rd = Third person sharing; S1 = 10% service charge; S2 = 15% service charge; BA = Private bath/shower; P = Pool; B = Beach on property or in vicinity; EP = European Plan (no meals); CP = Continental Plan (breakfast included); FAP = Full American Plan (all meals included); AI = All inclusive
NOTE: Rates (in US$) are given as a guideline only; price fluctuations can and will occur. Summer season generally runs 4/15–11/15 or 12/15; check with hotel concerned for specifics. Hotel tax is levied on each room regardless of the number of people staying in it.

| ADDRESS/ TELEPHONE | WINTER | | | SUMMER | | | | |
	S	D	ROOM TAX	S	D	ROOM TAX	# OF ROOMS	NOTES
The Belvedere Bch & City Hotel, 33 Gloucester Ave., Montego Bay, 952-0593/4	50–60	55–65	8	40–50	45–55	2	27	S2, BA, P, B, EP
Blue Harbour, Box 212, Montego Bay, 952-5445	Inquire		4	35–58	38–58	2	24	S1, BA, P, EP
Caribic House, White Sands PO, Montego Bay (1 Gloucester Ave.), 952-5013/4469	Inquire			27.50–44	35–50		14	S1, BA, EP
Cariblue Bch Hotel, Box 610, Montego Bay, 953-2022, 2250	45–50	65–72	8	40–45	50–55	4	17	S1, BA, P, B EP
Carlyle on the Bay, Box 412, Montego Bay (Kent Avenue), 952-4140/2	Inquire		4	Inquire		8	52	BA, P, B, AI
Casa Blanca Beach Club Box 469, Montego Bay, 952-0270/4866	98	156	8	79	118	4	57	S1, BA, P, B, AI
Chalet Caribe Hotel, Box 140, Spring Garden, Reading, St. James, 952-1364/5	Inquire		4	35	50	2	30	S1, BA, P, B, EP
Coral Cliff, Box 253, Montego Bay (Gloucester Avenue), 952-4130/1	Inquire		8	42–52	92–112	4	32	S1, BA, P, EP

Montego Bay Accommodations (*continued*)

	WINTER			SUMMER				
Comfort Guest House, Lot 55, Jarrett Terrace, Montego Bay 2, 952-1238	30	40		28	35		8	BA, B, EP
Chatwick Gardens, White Sands PO, Montego Bay (Queens Drive), 952-5491	Inquire		8	Inquire		4	26	S1, BA, P, B, EP
Doctor's Cave Beach Hotel, Box 94, Montego Bay (Gloucester Avenue), 952-4355	70–75 77–82 100–105	90–95 104–109 150–155	8	50–62 80–85	70–89 130–135	4	77	S1, BA, P, B, EP
Fantasy Resort, Box 161, Montego Bay (Gloucester Avenue), 952-4150/4	110–132	150–174	8	70	80	4	119	S1, BA, P, B, MAP
The Half Moon Club, Rose Hall, Box 30, Montego Bay, 953-2211	Inquire		12	100–120	130–150	8	203	S1, BA, P, B, EP
Harmony House Hotel, 27 Gloucester Ave., Montego Bay, 952-5710	Inquire		4	34	48–52	2	20	S1, BA, P, EP
Holiday House, Kent Avenue, Montego Bay, 952-2752/2934	70–80	75–85	8	Inquire		4	22	S1, BA, P, B
Holiday Inn, Box 480, Rose Hall, Montego Bay, 953-2485	117–141	244–296	10	75–99	80–104	6	516	BA, P, B, EP
Hotel Montego, Box 74, Montego Bay (Federal Avenue), 952-3286/7	Inquire		8	48	48	4	35	S1, BA, P, EP
Jack Tar Village, Box 144, Montego Bay (Gloucester Avenue), 952-4340	Inquire			180	280		128	BA, P, B, AI

Montego Bay Accommodations (*continued*)

	WINTER			SUMMER				
Jamaica Rose, White Sands PO, Montego Bay (427 Ferguson Ave., Ironshore), 952-1414	Inquire			135	270		9	BA, P, B, AI
La Mirage Hotel, 6 Queens Drive, Montego Bay, 952-4435/4637	Inquire		4	26–35	35–45	2	22	S1, BA, P, B, EP
Lady Diane Hotel, 5 Kent Avenue, Montego Bay, 952-4415	50	80	10	50	80	6	15	BA, P, B, EP
Life Styles Resort, Box 262, Montego Bay (Gloucester Avenue), 952-4703	Inquire			55	60		100	S1, BA, P, B, EP
Montego Bay Club Resort, White Sands PO, Montego Bay (Gloucester Avenue), 952-4310/4	78–112	90–112		Inquire			50	S1, BA, P, B, EP
Montego Bay Racquet Club, Box 245, Montego Bay (Sewell Avenue), 952-0200/3090	70	80		45	45		50	BA, P, EP
Ocean View Guest House, Box 210 Montego Bay (Sunset Avenue), 952-2662	24	32–36	4	19	27–51		12	S1, B
Pharos Villa, Box 26, Montego Bay (Pimento Hill, Reading), 952-3330	80	100		50	60		7	BA, P, B, EP
Ramparts Inn, 5 Ramparts Close, Montego Bay 1, 952-0200/3090	48–52	55–60		30–40	36–45		10	S1, BA, P, EP
Reading Reef Club Hotel, Box 225, Reading, St. James, 952-5909	100–185	150–205		67–90	94–125		21	BA, P, B, CP

Montego Bay Accommodations (*continued*)

	WINTER			SUMMER				
Richmond Hill Inn, Box 362, Montego Bay, 952-3859/2835	Inquire		8	Inquire		4	17	BA, P, CP
Ridgeway Guest House, Box 1237, Montego Bay (34 Queen's Drive), 952-2709	Inquire			25	45		4	BA, EP
Round Hill Hotel and Villas Box 64, Montego Bay (Hopewell, Hanover), 952-5150	225–400	260–305	4	145–155	180–190	8	107	BA, P, B, CP
Royal Court, Box 195, Montego Bay, 952-4531	Inquire		4	30–35	40–45	2	23	BA, P, B, EP
Sandals Resort Beach Club, Box 100, Montego Bay 1 (Kent Avenue), 952-5510/4	No rate	Inquire	10	No rate	1,825–2,350 pw		241	BA, P, B, AI
Sandals Royal Caribbean, Box 167, Montego Bay (Mahoe Bay), 953-2231/7	No rate	Inquire	10	No rate	1,825–2,350 pw		170	BA, P, B, AI
Sea Garden Beach Resort, Box 300, Montego Bay (Kent Avenue), 952-4780/1	411–431 (3 nights)	560–598 (3 nights)		318 (3 nights)	450 (3 nights)		100	BA, P, B, AI
Seawind Beach Resort, Box 1168, Montego Bay (Montego Freeport), 952-4070/2 952-4874/6	Inquire			60–70	152–168	4	430	S1, BA, P, B, EP
Seville Guest House, Box 1385, Montego Bay (Sunset Avenue), 952-2814/1984	Inquire			20	30	2	6	BA, B, EP

Montego Bay Accommodations (*continued*)

	WINTER			SUMMER				
Toby Inn Hotel, Box 467, Montego Bay (1 Kent Avenue), 952-4370	Inquire			50	65		65	S1, BA, P, EP
Trelawny Beach Hotel, Box 54, Falmouth, 954-2450/8	Inquire		8	99–110	146–162	10	350	S1, BA, P, MAP
Tryall Golf, Tennis, and Beach Club, Sandy Bay PO, Hanover, 952-5110	260–320	300–360	12	140–190	180–230	8	52	S1, BA, P, B, MAP
Verney House Hotel, Box 18, Montego Bay (3 Leader Avenue), 952-2875/1677	40–45	55–70	25	28–35	40–45	4	25	BA, B, EP
Wexford Court Hotel, 39 Gloucester Ave., Montego Bay	70–80	75–85	8	60–70	65–75	4	36	S1, BA, EP
Winged Victory Hotel, Box 333, Montego Bay (5 Queen's Drive), 952-3891/2	80–100		8	60–80	60–80	8	16	S1, BA, P, B, EP
Wyndham Rose Hall Beach Hotel, Box 999, Montego Bay, 953-2650/2617	Inquire		12	70–90	70–90	8	500	S1, BA, P, B, EP

Grove Restaurant inside the Doctor's Cave Beach Hotel. Others on Gloucester Avenue include the Cotton Tree Grill and Bar, Le Chalet, the Montegonian, Marguerite's by the Sea, Ma Maison, the Cascade Room at the Pelican, and the Wexford Grill. The Pier 1 Restaurant lies on the waterfront along Howard Cooke Blvd.. Elegant restaurants on Queen's Drive include the Diplomat, the Calabash, and the Gold Unicorn. The Club House Restaurant at Half Moon, Ironshore, and Evita's near Round Hill lie out of town. Also out of town is Le Cabaret which combines eating with watching (you guessed it) a cabaret performance. It's located at Hillcrams opposite the Holiday Inn. In-town restaurants include the Richmond Hill Inn on Union St., the Georgian House at the corner of Orange and

Union, the Town House at 16 Church St., the Rum Barrel Inn at 11 Market St., and Tradewinds at 47 Main St. The only Thai restaurant is the Siam at 25 Leader Avenue off Queen's Drive. The China Doll, 33 St. James St., and China Gate, 18 East St., serve Chinese food.

budget dining: Fortunately you don't have to spend a fortune to get fed, and you can get your stomach just as full with US$3 as with 30. Along the tourist strip, there's a snack and ice cream shop next to Doctor's Cave. A Shakey's Pizza (or, should it be called "A Shakey Excuse for Pizza"?) is across and down the street. Pa's Place has subs and Jamaican cuisine. A bit more expensive than in town but substantially cheaper than those surrounding it, Sunset Bar and Restaurant has local food. Once you get into town, there are innumerable hole-in-the-wall restaurants. The best way to find out what's available is to poke your nose in and ask. Tiger's, on Fort St. across from Woolworth's, has a great selection of cafeteria style food. It's a wonderful opportunity to see what you're going to be eating before you order it. What might be called the "Hard Rock Cafe of Mo Bay," Sub Machine has ice cream, spaghetti, fish and chips, submarine sandwiches, and fresh juices. Its black and white decor extends to the checks on the tile floor. Don't miss the framed wall posters. The boy is wearing oversized John Lennon sunglasses, and the girl has fishnet stockings on. All this and rhythm and blues while you munch. Capitol Snack, corner Barracks Rd. and Barnett St., has fried fish, delicious codfish and ackee sandwiches, pints of milk, pastries, etc. Lyle's Intensified is one of a few local restaurants down the street. Shazamm, "The Restaurant in a Snap," is one among many fast food restaurants. Located at Barnett St. and Bevin Ave., it serves chicken and ice cream. The Dome House at Union and Dome, serves jerk pork. There are a number of food markets including the Home Town Super on Church St. and a second-floor supermarket across from Doctor's Cave Beach.

entertainment: Most of the nightlife in this small town revolves around the tourist industry. There are occasional sessions at local clubs like the Del Caso, 13A Hart St. All-night reggae festivals also happen on occasion at Jarret Park. The only place with live music on a regular basis is Sir Winston's which features a caricature of a youthful Churchill on its marquee. Discos include Connections inside the Fantasy Resort, Thrillers Disco inside the Holiday Inn, and the Seawind Cave Disco at Seawind Beach Resort in Freeport. Siam Restaurant and Jazz Club, 25 Leader Avenue, presents live jazz Tues. through Sat. from 9 PM to midnight. The Cascade Bar inside the Doctor's Cave Beach Hotel features the Frank Smalling Duo (piano and drums) from Mon. through Thurs. nights and ballad singer/guitarist Horace Taylor entertains on Fri. evenings. The Belvedere offers live jazz on the last Sunday of each month. Cornwall Beach has sound system parties on Fri. nights, and Walter Fletcher has the same on Sun. evenings.

See films out under the stars at the Roxy, Barnett St.; a sign by the entrance reads NO RIPE BANANAS ALLOWED. Also try the Strand, Strand St., and the Palladium, Church St., where, on occasion live talent shows take place.

Incredibly brazen prostitutes ("mister, hey mister") hang out along the tourist strip.

events and festivals: First held in 1961, the Miami-to-Montego-Bay Yacht Race takes place in mid-February. Look for the Sugarcane Ball, a formal dance in aid of the Hanover Charities, which is held in mid-February at Round Hill. The Easter Tennis and Sports Spectacular usually is held at the beginning of April at the Wyndham Rose Hall. It features local and overseas tennis players competing and amateur golf and squash tournaments. The Easter Regatta held by the Yacht Club combines races with social events. A Culinary Arts Expo is held each July as part of the Independence Festival events. The Reggae Sunsplash, a week-long affair, features the top names in the business. It takes place every August at Bob Marley Performing Centre. Carib Tours and Red Stripe co-sponsor a professional and amateur golf tournament at the Half Moon Golf Club every November. Jonkanoo celebrations are held in the center of town each December.

shopping: City Shopping Center has a wide range of shops. There's also shopping (cruise-ship oriented) at Montego Freeport. The two straw markets in town cater to tourists, as do the numerous peddlers who line the streets from the General Post Office up through Doctor's Cave and vicinity. As far as shops go, as a general rule of thumb the further away from town you get, the higher the prices are. For example, a book which may sell for US$1 normally will sell for US$5 at a shop along the tourist strip. If buying from shops or from peddlers, always remember to bargain ferociously. Prices are bound to be higher during peak season. The best place to shop for crafts is the high quality "Things Jamaican" shop near the fort.

Charles Gordon Market: Located near the end of town on Fustic St.; turn R off Barnett when approaching from the center of town. Vendors spill out of all openings, overflowing up and down the street. At the entrance, men dispense medicines (Zion Searching Herb for worms, etc.) from metal shopping carts. Others sell in front of the VENDORS PROHIBITED sign. Inside, another man, again using a shopping cart, sells ice-cold ginger beer (J$0.80), beet, carrot, and soursop juices. Pandemonium reigns in another area of the packed market as a man wheels a shopping cart filled with freshly baked loaves of bread, a boy runs through shouldering stalks of sugarcane, another struts by selling small packages of dried beans from a basket, and a lady marches through selling shopping bags. The night unveils bingo games, and Kumina and Revival Zion prayer meetings. All of which does not seem to affect in the least the sleep of the female higglers curled up and collapsed in their portion of the octagonal concrete stalls.

services and information: Tourist Information is situated in an attractive complex in front of Cornwall Beach (open Mon. to Fri.; inquire about their Meet the People Program). Banks are located in Sam Sharpe Square. Open Mon. to Thurs 9–2; Fri. 9–12, 2–5. Change money (US$ and travelers cheques) in tourist shops. Count on getting J$0.30–0.50 or more per dollar above the bank rate. Note that if you change on the street, there's a chance of being ripped off or given counterfeit bills.

The G.P.O., located on Saint James St. (open 9–4:30, Mon. to Sat.), has a philatelic bureau. If picking up mail addressed to general delivery, count on a long, agonizing wait. Other post offices are at corner Barnett St. and Cottage Rd. and next to Doctor's Beach. The St. James Parish Library located across from the G.P.O., has a good collection of books on Jamaica in its reference section. Temporary membership cards are available. An American Consulate is located inside the Blue Harbour Hotel. For those requiring visa extensions, the Immigration Office is located on the third floor of Overton Plaza (open Mon. to Thurs. from 8:30–1, 2–5, and on Fri. from 8:30–1, 2–4.).

dealing with locals: The majority of people living here are friendly and hospitable. Be aware, however, that the "friendly" Jamaicans with nothing in their hands to sell you, as you walk through the strip area on the way to town, are selling their services as guides. They can show you the town or function as a "Star Wars" shield to protect you from other hustlers. If you think you might like a guide, get the price up front first. But they are really unnecessary. The only way to get rid of the hustlers is to ignore them. One favorite opening line they use is "Do you remember me?" Of course you don't because they've never laid eyes on you before. As with cultists or vacuum cleaner salesmen, once they have you in their clutches, they are almost impossible to get rid of. If you really want to meet some locals, try the "Meet The People" service offered by the tourist board.

Transport

getting around: It's possible to walk most places between the airport and Sam Sharpe Square. Minibuses and shared taxis that traverse the tourist strip to the airport and beyond leave from the side of Sam Sharpe Square along the road that leads to the straw market. Buses leave from the side of the straw market. Further down from the straw market to the south are the shared taxis going to the Freeport and Seawind

Beach Resort area. There are innumerable taxis which add a 25 percent surcharge between midnight and 5 AM. Check the yellow pages for a list of rental car companies. For bicycles on up to Honda 250 Rebels, try West Bike Rentals (tel. 952–0185), 27 Gloucester Avenue.

tours: Great River Productions (tel. 952–5047), 29 Gloucester Ave., has evening programs which include floor show, dinner, and dancing. Also at Great River, Evita's (tel. 952–2301/0100) has special events like cookouts and performances. With offices in Beach View Plaza, the Hylton High Tour (tel. 952–3343) takes you to a plantation for a continental breakfast, a roast suckling pig luncheon and a hot air balloon ride. Croydon (tel 952–4137), a pineapple and coffee plantation in the Cadalupa Mountains, also conducts tours. Mountain Valley Rafting (tel. 952–0527) has rafting tours down the Great River from Lethe. Many companies offer rafting on the Martha Brae near Falmouth. To visit the 200 acres of Chester Castle Great House, 14 mile W. in Hanover, contact Ian H. Cooke (tel. 952–3028). Accompong Tours (952–3539/0048) offers full-day tours to Accompong to visit the Maroons in the heart of Cockpit Country. Cambric Vacations (tel. 952–5013), Gloucester Ave., has a wide variety of tours in both English and German. Other tour companies include Amtrak (tel. 953–2774/2779) at Parkway Plaza, Rose Hall; Vacation Tours (tel. 952–5148/0728/3322), 2 Sunset Ave., Sunholiday Tours (tel. 952–5629, 952–4585), CCS Tours (tel. 952–6260), 15 East St., and Fun Time Vacation Tours (tel. 929-5394/5), 10 Ellesmere Rd..

trains, cruises, riding, and diving: The Catadupa Chu Chu (tel. 952–5919) wends its way to the S.E. A tour of Seaford Town is included. A similar set-up, The Governor's Coach Tour (tel 952–2887/1398), includes the chance to buy fabric at Catadupa and have it made into a suit or dress for pickup on the return portion of your journey. A tour of Ispwich Caves and a limbo contest are also included. Big Bird (952–2516/6347) offers a variety of catamaran cruises including a nude cruise set for Sunday mornings. Another catamaran, the Bamboo Prince (tel. 952–2163), offers cruises to a private beach as well as sunset cruises. A 55-foot old sailing ship, the *Calico* (tel. 952–

5860) offers snorkelling and sunset cruises. The ketch's claim to immortality is that it was featured in the 1985 Walt Disney flick "Return to Treasure Island." Rocky Point Stables (tel. 953–2286) at Half Moon Club features trail rides and lessons for adults and children. For diving call Poseidon Nemrod (tel. 952–3624), Montego Bay Divers (952–1414) at Freeport, and the Cariblue Beach Hotel (tel. 953–2180).

from Montego Bay: Minibuses leave from Creek St. for Negril and other west and southwest destinations. For Ochos Rios, Kingston, and the north coast, minibuses leave from the depot next to the craft market. Slow but full of local color, country buses meander down Barnett Street.

by train: A wonderfully slow, inefficient, but colorful and cheap way to get to Mandeville, Kingston and the more off-the-beaten-track destinations along the way is to board the trains departing daily. For Mandeville, get off in Williamsfield and take a shared taxi. Turn right at the Esso station on Barracks Rd. and go straight to find the train station.

by air: If you have a Jamaican Airlines ticket going through to Kingston, you'll have to pass through Immigration and Customs upon arrival there so have your passport ready. Trans Jamaican Airlines flies to Kingston, Negril, Ochos Rios, and Port Antonio. For reservations call 952–5401. Flights leave for many international destinations, including Miami, New York City, Port-au-Prince, Grand Cayman, Nassau and Caracas.

Vicinity of Montego Bay

heading south: Ms. Lisa Salmon's bird sanctuary is at Rocklands along the road to Anchovy. Tame birds will eat right out of your hand. (Open daily from 3 PM. Small admission fee charged.) An antiquated but still functioning water wheel at Tryall stands next to a golf course. Note the date 1834 inscribed along its base which indicates that the works were rebuilt after the 1832 slave rebellion. Perhaps the finest example of sugar estate ruins on the island, the mid-18th C. sugar factory at Kenilworth was constructed with great care. The shell of the H-shaped building stands next to the finely built Georgian water mill. The adjoining youth corps camp, patterned after the Civilian Conservation Corps, is well worth a visit.

heading east: The road in this direction is intermittently lined with hotels. Most famous attraction out this way is Rose Hall Great House. Take a local bus to get here; keep a sharp lookout for a white sign on the right. Open daily 9 AM-5 PM. Admission charged. Said to be the grandest 18th C. plantation house in the entire W. Indies, it has been restored to its former

Rose Hall Great House

grandeur by an American millionaire at a cost of US$2.5 million. Although it contains numerous 17th C. antiques and art treasures, most of these have been imported from abroad. There are many legends surrounding Annie Palmer, the "White Witch" of Rose Hall, who allegedly haunts the estate. One claims that she poisoned her first husband before going through another four. She also took on numerous slaves as lovers, murdering them as she tired of them. Finding her cruelty unbearable, slaves rebelled and murdered her in her bed in 1833. On Fri., 13 Oct. 1978, a crowd of 8,000 turned out to watch a team of psychics attempt to commune with her *duppy*. Bambos, a Greek Cypriot, received a psychic communication which led to the discovery of a huge termite mound containing a brass urn with a voodoo doll interred inside.

Greenwood Great House is further on. It has a collection of antique furniture and some rare musical instruments. Open daily 10 AM–6 PM. Admission charged.

FALMOUTH

Best preserved 18th C. town on the island, Falmouth still retains much of the Georgian style, in terms of harmony and symmetry, that it had at its zenith. Despite the valiant efforts of the Georgian Society, buildings continue to deteriorate, and those once roofed with shingles have been replaced with zinc. But the charm of the place is still very much intact. Old ladies still harness their mules in front of shops, goats still wander through the streets munching on shrubbery, and fishermen mend nets by the sea. Best time to visit is mid-afternoon when a sea breeze wafts over the main streets.

history: Founded at the end of the 18th C., the town flourished for less than 50 years before the prosperity of the sugar planters reached its peak. Given its name because Trelawny Parish's first governor was born in Falmouth, England, it became a free port in 1809. Its decline was due, in part, to the rise of Kingston as a commercial center, the increase in the size of ships which could no longer utilize its harbor, and the extension of the railroad to Montego Bay.

sights: Like early Kingston, Falmouth was laid out on a regular plan. Many scenes from the movie "Papillon" were filmed along Main Street. Numerous old buildings are grouped around central Water Square; less extensively renovated, however, are the ones along Market Street. Saint Peter's Church, Duke St., has a magnificent stained glass window. The old courthouse (1815) was remodeled after burning in the 1820s

Mending fishnets, Falmouth

and has never been the same since. William Knibb Presbyterian Church is dedicated to a man who was the most outspoken opponent of slavery on the island; his chapel was dubbed "Knibb's pestilential praying hole." On Emancipation Day in 1834, hundreds of slaves poured into town. At a nighttime ceremony, Knibb, speaking before an assembly at midnight, shouted, "The monster is dead. The Negro is free." As a part of the ceremony the shackles of slavery were buried in a coffin inscribed "Colonial Slavery died July 31, 1834 aged 276 years."

accommodations: The only hotel right in town is moderately priced Falmouth Resort (tel. 954–3391), 22 Newton St.. Trelawny Beach Hotel (tel. 954–2450/8), located on Rte. A1 well to the east of town, is a 350-room resort hotel with pool, beach and full sports amenities including tennis and golf. EP rates (not including 10 percent service charge) run US$143 s, $224 d during the winter and decrease to $103 s and $152 d during the off season. Carabatik (tel. 954–2314) has expensive guest bungalows. Villas can be rented at Silver Sands (tel. 954–2001) at Duncans to the east.

food: Glistening Waters restaurant (tel. 954–2229), located two miles east of Falmouth at Oyster Bay, is housed in what was originally a private clubhouse. Also try Fisherman's Club at the same location.

shopping: Check out Herbert Palmer's studio near the Shell station in town. Featuring the wax resist process of fabric dying which originated in Indonesia, Carabatik Fabrics, two miles to the east of Falmouth, offers locally produced specimens. Trelawny Book Supplies and Pharmacy is at 19 Market St..

sights in the vicinity and tours: Rafting on the Martha Brea river is the area's top tourist draw. Expect to pay about US$18 per raft for the hour trip if you arrange it through an agency. Two adults and a child can board a raft. On the banks of the river is the Good Hope Estate whose Great House dates from 1755. Lovingly restored, its grounds include water wheels, ruins, and a counting house. Horseback and plantation tours are by appointment (tel. 954–2289). Jamaican Swamp Safari, to the west of town, has tours daily on an hourly basis. The waters surrounding Glistening Waters Restaurant (tel. 954–3229/3138), at Oyster Bay to the east, glow in the dark with luminescence exuded from dinoflagellates. Twice-weekly boat tours are combined with dinner at the restaurant. Stewart Castle is a coastal estate a few km east of Falmouth which contains the remains of an unusual fortified house. It is currently the property of the Jamaica National Trust Commission. There's no charge to have a look; just ask the guard to open up for you. Windsor Cave to the south, one of the better-known caves on the island, is also one of the largest and most accessible. Many beautiful stalactites and stalagmites. Hampstead Estate contains the ruins of a factory, millpond, water tank and cattle mill.

Falmouth Harbour

DISCOVERY BAY

Originally known as Puerto Seco (Dry Harbor), the name of this small, largely middle-class community was changed to commemorate the spot where Columbus first landed. Someone made a mistake, however, because historians contend that he actually landed a few km west at Rio Bueno. The bauxite boom that took place in the '60s brought prosperity to this area, which has become a Jamaican version of American suburbia, complete with private beach and modest sports club. Except for a shopping center, post office and library, there's not much here save peace and quiet—a great place to unwind. A marine coral research center, run by the University of the West Indies, is just out of town along A1 to the west. Farther along the same road is a monstrously ugly bauxite terminal. Farther still is Columbus Park which has a great view and an outdoor museum which includes cannons, a water wheel, and a stone crest.

events: A carnival atmosphere prevails when the finals of the Push Cart Derby are held towards the end of August at the Kaiser Sports Club. Boys from 10 to 18 compete in their colorful home-engineered carts.

Vicinity of Discovery Bay

Rio Bueno: Take a minibus along A1 to the west and cross over Bengal Bridge (1798) and into Trelawny Parish where this miniscule but historic town is situated. Old warehouses, churches and Ft. Dundas here serve as a reminder of colonial times. Once an important port, it's now a quiet fishing village. Parts of the movie "A High Wind in Jamaica" were filmed on the main street. The two attractive churches here are the Rio Bueno Anglican Church (1883) and the Rio Bueno Baptist Church (1901). Fort Dundas (1778), at the end of the harbor, has been largely absorbed by the contiguous schoolyard. For an artistic touch to your day visit New Gallery Joe James, home of the painter and woodcarver. In case you're hungry, his small lunchroom serves lunch and dinner.

Brown's Town and vicinity: Take the road which heads north from the shopping plaza to Orange Valley Estate. This privately owned, 2,300-acre estate consists of an H-shaped great house, stone slave hospital, and boiling room with its 19th C. boiler added later. Sugar production ceased in these 18th C. buildings only in the middle of the 20th century. Arrange tours at the Estate Community Centre. Farther south are the grounds of Minard Estate which contains New Hope and Minard great houses. Centrally located at the junction of four main roads, Brown's Town is named after its founder, Irishman Hamilton Brown. This hilly country market town is one of the most pleasant Jamaican settlements. Meditation Height (tel.975-2588), a hotel which includes a restaurant and cocktail lounge, is located on Huntley Ave.. Country Life is an isolated and expensive eatery here. For food try Charley's Windsor House in Windsor House. Supa Save is at 32 Main St., as are RV Harris and Brown's Town Pharmacy. The market is held here on Sat. under the huge, tin-roofed outdoor market. Farther south near Alexandria is the "village" of Nine Miles, where Rastafarian reggae saint Bob Marley was born and lies buried. Decorated with flowers and pictures of Haile Selassie, his tomb is enshrined in a chapel atop a hillside. All-night memorial birthday concerts are held at this spot every February.

Runaway Bay

This area was the first planned resort to be developed for tourism during the 1960s with the opening of Cardiff Hall which is now a housing estate. Contrary to popular opinion, the people who ran away from what's now the resort area of Runaway Bay (whence its name), were African slaves fleeing to Cuba, not Spanish fleeing from the British. Touristic Runaway Caves and Green Grotto are in this area.

DISCOVERY BAY/RUNAWAY
BAY ACCOMMODATIONS

KEY: S = Single; D = Double; 3rd = Third person sharing; S1 = 10% service charge; S2 = 15% service charge; BA = Private bath/shower; P = Pool; B = Beach on property or in vicinity; EP = European Plan (no meals); CP = Continental Plan (breakfast included); FAP = Full American Plan (all meals included); AI = All inclusive
NOTE: Rates (in US$) are given as a guideline only; price fluctuations can and will occur. Summer season generally runs 4/15–11/15 or 12/15; check with hotel concerned for specifics. Hotel tax is levied on each room regardless of the number of occupants.

ADDRESS/ TELEPHONE	WINTER			SUMMER			# OF ROOMS	NOTES
	S	D	ROOM TAX	S	D	ROOM TAX		
Accommodationer, Box 89, Discovery Bay, 973-2559				37	37		7	BA, B, EP
Ambiance Jamaica Hotel, Box 20, Runaway Bay, 973-2066/7	95	96	8	50	60	4	74	S1, BA, P, B, EP
Caribbean Isle, Box 119, Runaway Bay, 973-2364	Inquire		4	35–45	45–55	4	23	S1, BA, P, B, EP
Eaton Hall Hotel & Villas, Box 112, Runaway Bay, 973-3404, 3503	125–170	190–250	10	75–105	105–134		52	S1, BA, P, B, MAP
Jamaica Jamaica—The Hotel, Box 58, Runaway Bay, St. Ann, 973-2436/8	Inquire			Inquire			238	BA, P, B, AI
Runaway H.E.A.R.T. Country Club Box 98, Runaway Bay, St. Ann, 973-2671/4	50	60		Inquire			20	S1, BA, P, B, EP
Silver Spray Resort, Box 16, Runaway Bay, 973-3413, 2006	50–75	65–75		40	50		16	S1, BA, P, EP
Tamarind Tree Resort Hotel, Box 235, Runaway Bay, 974-5337	41	50		34.80	44.70		10	S1, BA, B, EP

accommodations: A number of resorts are located in the vicinity. The most reasonably priced is Tamarind Tree Beach Resort. See chart for details. For longer stays, contact Del Bar Apartments (tel. 973–2335). For those on a tight budget, check around in Discovery Bay.

villas: For information on renting villas and the like call the local branch of the Jamaica Association of Villas and Apartments (JAVA) at 973–2356. Also contact Sunflower Beach Resort and Villas (tel. 973–2171/2173), Box 150, Runaway Bay. Also contact Paddy Morris (tel. 973–2317), Box 92, Discovery Bay. The three bedrooms of Runaway Bay Villa may be reserved by calling (416) 281-3228 in Toronto.

food: Open daily, Northern Shopping complex, which sells everything from jerk pork to ice cream to fried chicken, is in Salem to the east. Charley's Inn, also at Salem, specializes in lobster thermidor. Also try the unusually named El Africano Midway Drive-In Club on Main St. (jerk pork!) and Bird Wind Restaurant and Cocktail Lounge which is open from 9 AM to midnight. The numerous tourist hotels also serve meals. For food shopping try A & B Supermarket and W & R Super Saves at Columbus Plaza; Clarke's Green Grocery is on Main St.; also try Taylor's Supermarket.

events: Runaway Bay's Golf Club hosts an amateur golf competition during Independence Week.

heading east from Runaway Bay: Near the Columbus Monument and Seville great house, are the ruins of Sevilla La Nueva, abandoned after the Spanish left for the greener pastures of Spanish Town in 1534—just 24 years after its founding. Nothing remains of the original settlement save archaeological ruins which are being excavated with the goal of establishing a major cultural and historical center here in time for the 500th anniversary in 1992 of Columbus's first voyage. A search is currently underway for Columbus's two caravals which were beached and abandoned here in 1503–04. Capital of St. Ann's Parish, the village (pop. 8,000) of St. Ann's is just a bit farther down the road. Besides being the birthplace of national hero Marcus Garvey, it is notable for its his-

toric courthouse (1860) and fort. Used until recently as a
slaughterhouse, St. Ann's Bay Fort was built in 1750 of stone
blocks hauled from the ruins of Sevilla La Nueva. A scene
from the film "Dr No" was shot at Cotter's Wharf.

For food try Square 1, which has local dishes, snacks, and burgers, at 7 Bravo St., Drax Hall, which houses St. Ann's Polo
Club, holds matches every Sat. at 4 PM. There's also a small
craft village here.

Due south of St. Ann, at Pedro between Claremont and Kellits,
stand the ruins of the small storied house equipped with circu-
lar towers, known as Edinburgh Castle. Here lived the "mad
doctor" Lewis Hutchinson, the infamous 18th C. mass mur-
derer. Perhaps as many as 40 travelers over the years were
shot, robbed, and decapitated while his slaves stood silent wit-
ness. Discovered after he shot a neighbor, Hutchinson was captured while attempting to flee by ship. Before being hanged in
Spanish Town in 1773, he willed 100 pounds for the construction of a monument whose epitaph would have read: "Their
sentence, pride, and power I defy. Despise their power, and like
a Roman I die." Needless to say, it was never erected.

OCHO RIOS

Unlike other north coast towns, which have regressed from
bustling ports into quiet fishing villages, Ocho Rios has done
just the opposite, metamorphosing from a sleepy fishing village into a bustling tourism and bauxite shipping center. If
you're in search of unspoiled Jamaica, you won't find it here.
Unlike Montego Bay, Ocho Rios is a planned tourist resort.
The government-owned St. Ann Development Company acquired land in the Ochos Rios area during the 1960s, dredged
the harbor, and reclaimed the white sand beach. The name
Ocho Rios is a corruption for the Spanish word *chorreros*
("waterfall"); the Spanish gave this stretch of coastline the
name because of the large number of waterfalls (now mostly
tapped for hydroelectricity) which line this coast.

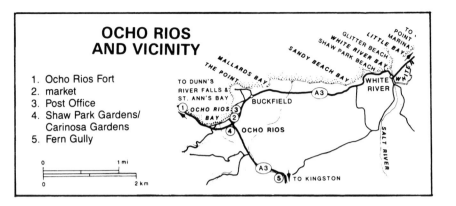

OCHO RIOS AND VICINITY

1. Ocho Rios Fort
2. market
3. Post Office
4. Shaw Park Gardens/ Carinosa Gardens
5. Fern Gully

getting there: Direct minibuses run from Montego Bay and Kingston. From Port Antonio it's necessary to change several times unless you take one of the country buses leaving early in the morning. Departing Kingston between 7:30 and 8 AM, Econotours' Ocho Rios Shuttle (tel. 24922,27538) charges US$20 pp.. Trans Jamaican flies from Montego Bay, Kingston, and Port Antonio into Boscobel to the east of town.

sights: The latest if rather high priced attraction is Carinosa Gardens located above town. It covers 20 acres of waterfalls and hanging gardens with 200 varieties of orchids and 300 species of ferns. Other vegetation includes cacti, bromelia, hibiscus, lilies, and many others. Enter the walk-in aviary and have 200 species of birds flutter above your head. In addition, a seawater aquarium contains over a thousand tropical fish.

Ochos Rios Fort stands outside of town to the west next to Reynold's bauxite installation. Recently rebuilt by Reynold's Jamaica, the late 17th C. fort contains two original cannon and two borrowed from Mammee Bay. One of the most famous and popular attractions in Jamaica, Dunn's River Falls are on a paved road off to the south. Open from 9 to 6, there's a J$2 entrance fee with an additional J$1 charge to climb the falls. Guides depend upon tips for their income. Your guide will help you climb and carry your gear as you slip and slide all along the way to the top of this gently sloping waterfall. A bathing beach, snack bar, and toilets are located at its base where the

Carinosa Gardens

water tumbles into the ocean. The battle of Los Chorreros was fought near this spot, in which the English defeated the Spanish Expeditionary Force from Cuba. Much more private and less frequented is the waterfall one mile farther west at the hydroelectric station.

accommodations: Centrally located, the Hibiscus Lodge Hotel doesn't seem like much when you first approach. As you descend through the garden, however, you find a tennis court, a swimming pool with fountains spurting over the water, a jacuzzi, and swinging hammocks. The theme is white—white lattice work and white fences. All of this is suspended above

Dunn's River Falls

the gently rippling waters of the Caribbean. And one of the best snorkeling areas in the Caribbean lies below. A staircase, housing caged tropical birds in an alcove to the side, leads down to it. Swiss managed, the hotel includes its own labeled soap and matches, and it even sells its own label of rum. All in all, it's remarkably quiet, relaxing, and peaceful. There are also innumerable other hotels listed by the Tourist Board. The most famous luxury hotels are Jamaica Inn and the Sans Souci. See chart for rates. Other hotels not listed by the Tourist Board include River Sea Inn on Main St.; Big Daddy's Motel and Pier View Apartments (974–2607), 19 Main St; Hunter's Inn (974–5627), 86 Main St., and Marine View Hotel and Club (974–5753), 9 James Ave.

villas: The headquarters of Jamaica Association of Villas and Apartments (JAVA/tel. 974–2508), is in Pineapple Place. Try Jeanne Dixon Real Estate (tel. 974–5187/2359), 154 Main St., and Sunshine Jamaica, Box 335 Ocho Rios (tel. 974–2980). To rent room(s) in a three-bedroom villa with kitchen and swimming pool near Galina to the east, contact Idris Ackamoor, 741 Elizabeth St., San Francisco, CA or write c/o 19 Idewild Crescent, PO Box, Galina, St. Mary.

budget accommodations: You really have to use your nose and sniff around here. Locals may approach you offering a room. The best deal for campers and those on a budget is out at aptly named Hummingbird Haven just past Jamaica Inn. Audrey Barnett and Peter Hudson have opened their home and their hearts to visitors. They have one fan-equipped room available inside their house with a double bed which rents for US$20 per night including breakfast. The bath is shared. Two modest cabins containing detached twin beds, fan, and private bath rent for $28 each per night. Campers are charged $5 per tent site pn for up to two persons. Brooklyn Inn (up the road past Sandals) has reasonably priced but not wonderful rooms; road noise could be a problem.

dining out: Extremely popular is The Almond Tree which is noted for its atmosphere, lobster, and literally "flaming" dishes. The Ruins, which is Chinese managed, is also famous; it features seafood, steak, chicken, and mainstays of American Chinese cooking like Chow Mein and Chop Suey. Carinosa Gardens, above the town, features luncheon dishes like Bay Marlin Smoked and Seville Chicken Julienne, and dinner entrees like Shrimps Caribe in Bay Sauce and Fillet Tournedos Carinosa. Carib Inn and the Little Pub Restaurant are on Main Street. Casanova Restaurant, featuring seafood, pasta,

OCHO RIOS ACCOMMODATIONS

KEY: S = Single; D = Double; 3rd = Third person sharing; S1 = 10% service charge; S2 = 15% service charge; BA = Private bath/shower; P = Pool; B = Beach on property or in vicinity; EP = European Plan (no meals); CP = Continental Plan (breakfast included); FAP = Full American Plan (all meals included); AI = All inclusive
NOTE: Rates (in US$) are given as a guideline only; price fluctuations can and will occur. Summer season generally runs 4/15–11/15 or 12/15; check with hotel concerned for specifics. Hotel tax is levied on each room regardless of the number of people staying in it.

ADDRESS/ TELEPHONE	WINTER			SUMMER			# OF ROOMS	NOTES
	S	D	ROOM TAX	S	D	ROOM TAX		
Arawak Inn, Arawak P.O., Mammee Bay, 972-2318	34–38		8	29	29	2	17	S1, BA, B, P, EP
Briscobel Bch Hotel, Box 63, Ocho Rios, 974-3330/7	Inquire			Inquire			181	BA, B, P, AI
Club Americana, Box 100, Ocho Rios, 974-2151/9	Inquire			1,028–1,238 pw	1,364–1,572		325	BA, P, B, AI
Couples (Tower Isle), Box 330, Ocho Rios, 974-3330/7	Inquire			Inquire			152	BA, P, B, AI
Eden II, Box 51, Ocho Rios, 972-2382/6	Inquire			900–1760 pw			263	BA, B, P, AI
Hibiscus Lodge Hotel (Main Street), Box 52, Ocho Rios, 974-2676	Inquire		8	44	64	4	26	S1, BA, P, B
Inn on the Beach, Box 342, Ocho Rios, 974-2782/4	66	82	8	53	60	4		S1, BA, B, EP
Jamaica Inn, Box 1, Ocho Rios, 974-2514	250	300–350	12	135	180–205	8	90	S1, BA, B, P, MAP

and other Italian cuisine, is found at the Sans Souci. Glenn's Restaurant at Tower Cloisters, Tower Isle in town, has Jamaican cuisine, lobster, and steak. Dick Turpin (named after the outlaw) is in the Coconut Grove Shopping Center. Beach Bowl

Ocho Rios Accommodations (*continued*)

	WINTER			SUMMER				
Little Pub Inn, Box 256, Ocho Rios (59 Main St), 974-2324	42.73	85.46		30	30		22	S1, BA, B, CP
Mallards Bch Hotel, Box 254, Ocho Rios, 974-2201	120–140	130–150	12	80–100	90–105	8	370	S1, BA, B, P, EP
Pineapple Penthouse Hotel, Box 263, Ocho Rios, 974-2727	40	50	4	30	80	2	25	S1, BA, B, P, EP
Plantation Inn, Box 2, Ocho Rios, 974-5601	Inquire		12	135–250	155–270	8	77	S1, BA, B, P, CP
Sandals Ocho Rios, Main St., Ocho Rios, 974-5453	Inquire			Inquire			237	P, BA, B, AI
Sans Souci Hotel, Club & Spa, Box 103, Ocho Rios, 974-2353	220–260	240–400	12	115–155	135–175		71	S1, BA, B, P, AI
Shaw Park Beach Hotel, Box 17, Ocho Rios, 974-2552/4	138–151	150–163	10	96–108	107–121	6	118	S1, BA, B, P, CP
Silver Seas Hotel, Box 81, Ocho Rios, 974-2755	88–108	96–136	10	60	70	6	80	S1, BA, B, EP
Turtle Bch Towers, Box 73, Ocho Rios, 974-2801/5, 2646	97	220–240		70–78	76–116	8	120	S1, BA, B, P, EP

is at Ocean Village Shopping Centre. Mallards Beach Hotel has The Pimento Room, an a/c coffee shop, and Garden Terrace and Patio. Palm Beach Restaurant has an assortment of steak and seafood. Blue Cantina, 81 Main St., serves dishes like Mexican tacos, curried goat, chicken, steak, and burgers. Palm Beach Restaurant, next to Inn on the Beach, has French style cuisine from around US$12. Le Gourmand at Coconut Village also serves French cuisine. Sea Pearls, specializing in seafood and local dishes, is at 87 Main St.. Tradewinds Patio Restaurant features a wide variety of seafood. Outside of town to the east eight miles lies Moxon's of Boscobel where you dine by candlelight overlooking the sea. Arawak Garden Restaurant, located inside the Arawak Inn at Mammee Bay to the west, specializes in seafood. Marsh Farms, situated at retreat in St. Mary, serves a Jamaican buffet on Tuesdays and Thursdays.

budget dining: The Coffee Shop, near Burger King, has cups of freshly brewed High Mountain and Blue Mountain coffee. For the same you can also try The Blue Mountain Coffee Place. At Ocean Village, Chuckle Berrys has ice cream, as does the straightforwardly named Mark's Pastry and Ice Cream. Baked goodies are also available at Honey Bee Pastry Shop. Shakey's Pizza serves breakfast daily from 7:30 in an unusually pleasing environment for a fast food restaurant. They also serve chicken and spaghetti. The ubiquitous Burger King and Kentucky Fried complete the fast food landscape. Ocho Rios Jerk Centre, on Main St. opposite Turtle Towers, features jerk pork, chicken, fish, and spare ribs. The Cafeteria in front of The Ruins restaurant is much more reasonable than its neighboring namesake. Moderately priced local food is served at Parkway Restaurant in town. Regal Restaurant is at the Clock Tower. Licosa Cafe inside the Shell station serves local food. The Lobsterpot Restaurant, Main St., serves very reasonably priced local food in an attractive venue. Jeff's, next door at 10 Main St., also has moderate prices. The Munch Wagon in town serves everything from Jamaican cuisine to ice cream. The Tropical Fruit Basket, just past Carib Arcade, heading east, serves everything from tropical fruit juices to fish and bammy and fish and chips. Many bakeries are in town near the market as are some other small restaurants. Food Fair is a small supermarket at Ocean Village. Family Fair and Budget supermarkets are nearby at 14 and 18 Main St. respectively; Chen's is at 78 Main St.; Rexo Supermarket is in New Ocho Rios Plaza. Further out to the east are Auntie's Grocery and Willie's Variety & Grocery at 130 Main St.. The large and dynamic town market is liveliest on Thursdays.

entertainment: There's not much going on except at the big hotels. If you hear the sounds of a session in progress, let your feet follow your ears. You'll find locals twisting their hips along to the riddims blaring out of huge banks of speakers. Goat's Head Soup is usually on sale. Top local joint is the Club

Up Session at 7 James Ave.. Just look for the flashing beacon set atop a pyramid and Christmas-style lighting. Beautiful young Jamaican women will open a locked gate to let you in and collect the J$10 cover. Live music—with resident band The Town Moor playing dub versions of tunes like "Norwegian Wood"—usually begins at around 9:30 PM on Friday through Sunday nights. A painted notice reads "No Pross, No Drugs, No Pimps." Soca tunes compete for air time across the street upstairs at Ocean Villa. For the older and more laid back but still active, sentimental R&B standards play over a system weekend evenings at the Jerk Pork Centre. Bill's Place combines a seductively romantic atmosphere with card and dice games. Cozier and featuring higher priced original drinks, the bar at the Hibiscus Lodge Hotel features swinging bar chairs mounted on ropes. Dedicatedly brazen hookers hang in front of the Love Club, a go go joint with bikini-clad dancers in town. Shakey's Pizza has pitchers of Red Stripe on sale evenings from 9 to midnight. Say "hi" to Percy their terminally bored parrot. The movie theater has cheap double and triple features in which Cher may share the bill with King Fu. In season check to see which of the hotels have live bands; the Little Pub Inn is particularly noted for this. You might also want to check out Footprints at Coconut Grove Shopping Centre or the Apple Disco at the Arawak Inn at Mammee Bay.

events: Harmony Hall holds a number of exhibitions during the year as well as craft fairs before Easter and Christmas and an anniversary show every November. Chukka Cove holds a polo tournament every January and the Redstripe International Polo Tournament and Horse Show every April.

shopping: The majority of shops in town are located at Ocean Village. They include Vibes Music; The Craft Cottage, which features local crafts including stuffed dolls; Mickey's Children's Store, featuring goods for aspiring adults; Everybody's Bookshop; and The Collection, which has batik. The Music Centre lies across from the Texaco station. The Methodist Church runs a small craft shop at the rear of the school. Although the shop itself isn't particularly notable, it's worth a visit just to peer into the school which is like a small one-room open-air museum of Jamaican primary education. Ocho Rios Craft Park has an extensive range of goodies, as does Old Market Craft Shoppes near Ocean Village; there are also shops in the large market. If braided hair constitues a "souvenir," then women may wish to take home a custom crocheted head from Braider's Village which features 20 experienced "hair weavers." Rochemar Books and Sports is at 75D Main St.. Shops in The Duty Free Shopping Centre sell alcohol, crystal goods, etc.. The Thrift Centre has a collection of tee shirts for J$22. Coconut Joe has an unusual collection of tee shirts including one of the ever present Saint Robert Nesta. Pineapple Place, to the east of town on the left, has a large number of shops including a small record store and a straw market to the rear and side. Further on to the right, Coconut Grove Shopping Centre has the usual including Bette's Handmade Batik & Tie Dye and yet *another* straw market, this time featuring small

Ocho Rios

yellow and white houses. Finally, don't forget the art gallery at Harmony Hall.

services and sports: The post office and banks are on Main St.. Tourist Board office is inside Ocean Village Shopping Centre. The library is on Milford Rd. on the way to Fern Gully. Ocho Rios Pharmacy is at the clocktower. Central Medical Labs Ltd. (tel. 974–2614) is at 14 Carib Arcade. Other pharmacies include Great House Pharmacy at Brown's Plaza and Pine Grove Pharmacy at Pineapple Place. The Laundry Mart dry cleaners are next to the River Sea Inn and the Lobster Inn restaurant. For those who wish to try to get into shape in a day or two or who are fraught with guilt about missing their regular fitness workout schedule, the Sans Souci's small Nautilus-type facility, stationary bicycles, tennis court, cold water mineral spring pool, swimming pool, and detached beach, are available for use by the public at $US10 per day. Chukka Cove (tel. 972–2506), at Richmond, Llandovery, St. Ann, is the island's premier equestrian facility. Garfield Diving Station (tel. 974–4420), located to the west of Mallard Beach Hotel, offers deep sea fishing, snorkeling, cruises, diving, and other water sports.

tours: These include Dunn's River Cruise; Dunn's River Feast (a buffet followed by nighttime climb of the falls, folklore performance, a fashion show, and reggae dancing); and Night on the White River which features a folkloric show. Shaw Park Gardens has a tea on Tuesdays followed by a fashion show and band concert. Tours and horseback riding are available daily at Prospect Plantation, Ocho Rios. Call 974–2058 to reserve. The Coconut Grove Great House (tel. 974–2619), back behind Coconut Village Shopping Centre, also features twice weekly reggae parties which begin with dinner. Heading back to the west, Circle B Farm (in Liberty District near Priory, St. Ann on the way to Runaway Bay) offers tours and a buffet lunch. In the Ocho Rios vicinity, Brimmer Hall Estate and Friendship Farm also have tours.

dealing with locals: These days Ocho Rios is more filled with bustle than hustle. Although the latter is still present in abundance, it's not as extreme as in Negril and Montego Bay.

Post office near Ocho Rios

The worst area is around the market. Since the beach charges for entry and the hotels generally restrict use to guests, things are a lot calmer.

from Ocho Rios: Buses and minibuses leave for all points from the vicinity of the clocktower and the Shell station.

Vicinity of Ocho Rios

To the south along A3 just outside of town are the ornately landscaped Shaw Park Gardens. A bit farther is Fern Gully. Of obscure origin but thought to have been planned out by a Superintendent of Public Gardens in the 1880s, the vegetation here has been decimated several times since then by floods and hurricanes. In fact it is still recovering from 1988's Hurricane Gilbert.

Six and a half km (four miles) to the east stands Harmony Hall, an old house (1896) which has been transformed into an art gallery, craft center and pub-restaurant.

At Rio Nuevo visit the battle site where the Spanish defeated the British. It's open daily from 9 AM to 4 PM. Stewart's Town, a small village nearby, is notable for Moxon's, a gourmet restaurant, and Lloyd's Ceramics.

Near Oracabessa is Firefly, Noel Coward's home. Difficult to reach on a 305-m-high plateau, it has been immaculately preserved and transformed into a museum. Longtime housekeeper Imogene Frazier now acts as a tourguide. Preserved

View from Noel Coward's house, Port Maria

almost as he left it, the interior contains his paintings, two pianos, writing desk, and other such memorabilia. Closed Tues. and Thursday. A short distance down the road is Golden Eye, the home of Ian Fleming. Here he wrote many of his famous James Bond novels. The house is closed to the public.

Port Maria: Capital of St. Mary's Parish, this small town, stretched out along two bays strewn with huge rocks which separate them, was once a bustling banana port. The sign reading TO THE TACKY MONUMENT does not, as the name suggests, lead to a tacky, tasteless monument but rather to one dedicated to Jamaican freedom fighter Tacky who led a slave insurrection in 1760. This rebellion, brutally put down by the authorities, was led by "Coromantees" or slaves from Ghana's Asante warrior tribe. Ruins of Ft. Haldane stand near Gray's Charity at the edge of town. Frontier is an old estate at the east end of the bay which is where Tacky's revolt originated.

AROUND THE
EAST COAST

PORT ANTONIO

A small town perched above two natural harbors, Port Antonio
is perhaps the most beautiful settlement in all Jamaica: the
location and setting couldn't be more perfect. The surrounding
Portland Parish scenery is magnificent, with white sand
beaches and small, classic islands just off the shoreline. The
town itself is compact without being claustrophobic. Its easy-
going atmosphere contrasts dramatically with the island's
other resort towns.

getting there: Take any bus or minibus from Kingston to
Annotto Bay. No through minibuses leave from Ocho Rios so
you must change along the way at Port Maria and Annotto
Bay. While waiting at the latter, you may enter the doorway of
the local library and read magazines to find out what was
happening four years ago. If planning to go straight through
from Montego Bay, be sure to leave early.

Trans Jamaica also flies from Kingston, Montego Bay and
Ocho Rios.

history: Although the first British settlers attempted to
change the name to Titchfield, the original name of the small
Spanish settlement, Puerto Anton, prevailed in the end. In
order for the British to maintain their grip on this corner of
the island where slaves far outnumbered overseers, land

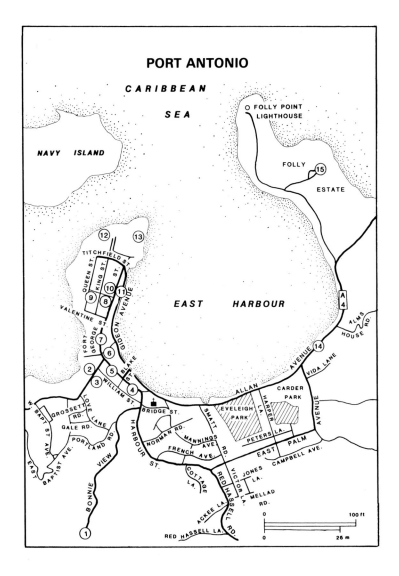

PORT ANTONIO

CARIBBEAN SEA

FOLLY POINT LIGHTHOUSE

NAVY ISLAND

FOLLY

ESTATE

EAST HARBOUR

TITCHFIELD ST.

TITCHFIELD

QUEEN ST.

KING ST.

VALENTINE ST.

FORT GEORGE ST.

GIDEON AVENUE

BLAKE ST.

WILLIAM ST.

LOVE LANE

GROSSETT RD.

GALE RD.

W. BAPT ST. AVE

EAST

BAPTIST AVE.

PORTLAND RD.

HARBOUR VIEW RD.

BONNIE VIEW

HARBOUR ST.

BRIDGE ST.

NORMAN RD.

MANNINGS AVE.

FRENCH AVE.

SMATT RD.

EVELEIGH PARK

ALLAN LA.

HARPER LA.

PETERS LA.

CARDER PARK

EAST PALM

CAMPBELL AVE.

VIDA LANE

AVENUE

AVENUE

HOUSE RD.

LMS RD.

COTTAGE LA.

RED HASSELL RD.

VICTOR LA.

JONES LA.

MELLAD RD.

ACKEE LA.

RED HASSELL LA.

0   100 ft

0   25 m

1. Bonnie View Hotel
2. bus station
3. market
4. Hope View Guest House
5. City Centre Plaza (Tourist Information)
6. Court House/Post Office
7. Delmar Theater
8. DeMontevin Guest House
9. Scotia Guest House
10. The Rose
11. Ms. Peggy's Place
12. Jamaica Reef Beach
13. Titchfield School
14. Stop Brap Restaurant
15. Folly Ruins
16. Navy Island Ferry

Port Antonio, from Bonnieview

grants were offered to settlers from Europe, and the town was laid out. To protect the settlers, Fort George was constructed on Titchfield Peninsula, and Navy Island was renamed and fortified. Bananas from the Canary Islands, introduced to Jamaica by way of Hispaniola by the Spaniards, were scorned as being food fit only for animals. It never occurred to the Jamaicans to export them, until entrepreneur Capt. Lorenzo Dow Baker discovered the profit in shipping to New England when he made US$2000 delivering an unripened boatload in 1871. Baker started and built up the Boston Fruit Company, which merged with the United Fruit Company in 1939. The U.F.C. monopoly lasted for a few years thereafter, until it was broken, partly by the effects of Panama Disease on the banana crop and partly by competition from the newly formed Jamaica Banana Producer's Association. Since then, exports have shifted toward Britain and quantities have declined. One day in 1947, Errol Flynn, sailing in on his yacht *Zacca*, discovered the town and decided to make it his home. Moving quickly, he purchased the Titchfield Hotel (which he renamed the Jamaica Reef), and Navy Island just off the coast. Largely because of this presence, Port Antonio became the "in" place for the rich and powerful in the 1950s. Some of this glamour remains today in the form of the villas which line the roads around the Blue Hole. The town's romantic legacy was revitalized in 1988 with the arrival of a film crew to do a remake of *The Lord of the Flies.*

Sights

Best way to get oriented is to take the steep road up Richmond Hill to Bonnie View Hotel which commands a perfect view of the bay below. Magnificent place to watch sunsets. From the center of town follow Fort Saint George St. to the end and turn left to find the ruins of Errol Flynn's Jamaica Reef Hotel. A path to the left leads to a small beach. What was once the exclusive property of the rich is now—thanks to a fire—the property of all. A pleasant spot to sit and meditate. Hurry and get here before some developer moves in and builds again. Look for banana boats departing from here. What little remains of Fort St. George has been built into the Titchfield School at the same end of the peninsula. At the other end of town, just on the left side of the road heading east, turn left on a side road marked by two empty sentry boxes and a JAMAICA FOR JESUS sign. Follow this road up and enter Folly Estate. In 1905 Alfred Mitchell from New London, Connecticut, had this mansion built, but his wife refused to live in it. He lived here off and on until he died in 1912. In 1938 the roof fell in because the iron reinforcement rods had been corroded by sea salt. Acquired by the government in 1949, it was leased to Mrs. Errol Flynn for construction of a resort, but this project fell through. And so it remains today—a ruined concrete and limestone mansion with a winding staircase to the top, sexually explicit graffiti scrawled on the side, and Doric pillars cast from concrete. From the beach below swim or wade over to Wood Island just offshore. Despite the name, there are but two palms and a few other trees for shade. The roof of this mansion

Port Antonio downtown

would be a perfect place to take in the full moon or stargaze. Other buildings are scattered over the plain with a few in front of the entrance to the small red-and-white striped light-house. Continue down the road until you reach an imposing structure looming off on the headland. Yes, it is a castle, and, yes, you are still in Jamaica. Modeled on a Bavarian medieval castle, its construction was ordered by a German baroness. Progress halted, one story has it, when she was found to be smuggling funds out of the country illegally. Between 1980 and 84, it was known as Folly II and seemed fated to a similar end as its predecessor. The construction site was rescued from decrepitude in 1984 by architect Earl Levy, and it now lacks

Folly Estate

only charging knights in armor carrying off fair maidens to complete its authenticity. To one side of the "castle," rough coral bluffs engage in combat with the sea as the waves clash and recede. Definitely a location to visit when it's thundering and a storm is brewing. A few km farther down the road is San San Beach (admission charged). One of the prettiest beaches on the north coast, it's often nearly deserted on weekdays, even in peak season. The only catch is that there are a lot of sea urchins. Monkey Island (also know as Pellew I.) is visible from the shore of San San. Covered with colorful vegetation, it no longer has any monkeys. Next beach along the road is Fairy Hill Beach at Winnifred which has changing rooms and showers. One of the area's most famous tourist attractions, the Caves of Nonsuch and Gardens of Athenry, lie to the southeast. Guided tours (993–3740) are available from 9–5:30 daily.

Blue Hole and beyond: The legendary Blue Lagoon or Blue Hole is farther down the road past Monkey Island, J$1.20 by minibus (scarce in the evening). Turn left off the main road

Monkey Island

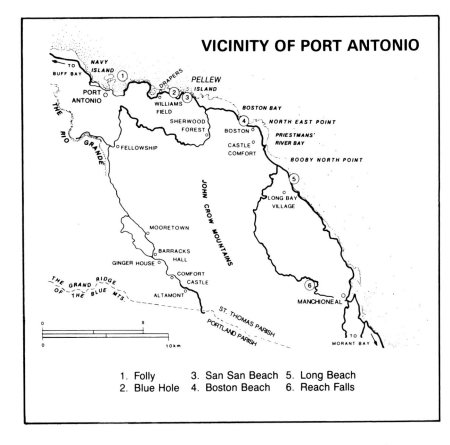

VICINITY OF PORT ANTONIO

1. Folly   3. San San Beach   5. Long Beach
2. Blue Hole   4. Boston Beach   6. Reach Falls

and follow the sloping, flower-wreathed road leading to it.
Quiet and serene, this beautiful spot is composed of a mixture
of salt- and freshwater released from underground streams.
Dropping off sharply from near the shoreline, the bottom
plummets to a depth of 65 m (210 ft.), which accounts for its
intense, emerald-green clarity. Bring your own lunch and
some bread for feeding the fish. There's a quite romantic restaurant right at the edge of the lagoon. The entire area surrounding Blue Lagoon contains the island's most deluxe hotels
and villas. Trident, Frenchman's Cove and Jamaica Hill are
among those which charge US$200 per night with two meals.
Boston Beach, a small but beautiful beach set between tower-

Blue Hole

ing cliffs, is farther down the road. The area around this beach is famous all over Jamaica for its jerk pork. Locals here learned to make it from the Maroons. A few km east of Boston Bay lies the ranch of Mrs. Errol Flynn, where she resides along with 2,000 head of cattle. Still farther is the less frequented and more spacious Long Bay, with its immaculate beach. The only action out this way is Sir Pluggy's Jerk Chicken and Bamboo Lawn, a local restaurant which has movies on Monday nights.

To see the Sam Street Collection of African Art near Long Bay, take a right at Fair Prospect and go up the hill past Fair Prospect Secondary School passing through the districts of Hartford and Connecticut, then turn right into a driveway at the top of the hill to find a house constructed on the ruins of an old fortress. While the collection is dilapidated and poorly housed, it's definitely worth seeing.

Reach Falls, small, exquisite, and relatively untouristed, has been acclaimed as the most beautiful spot in Jamaica. Turn right one and a half km (one mile) after Machioneal and follow the rough road for three km (two miles) until you come to a fork which leads there. A group of self-appointed maintenance men will try to hit you for a fee. Pay if you like.

heading west: Rafting trips on the Rio Grande, a touristic diversion invented by Errol Flynn, start at a base near Berrydale. It's a three-hour trip with pauses for photos and swimming. Vendors appear around the bend at intervals with cold Red Stripes. You'll have to take a taxi to the departure point and back again from Rafter's Rest. For the best price, bargain with the raftsmen who hang out on Harbour St. across from the post office. Eleven km (seven miles) west is Somerset Falls. A lush garden surrounds the lower falls; the larger one lies at the end of a narrow gorge accessible by swimming or raft. Admission is J$2 which includes the raft trip.

Rafting, Rio Grande River

Navy Island: Originally named Lynch Island, after one of Jamaica's early governors who was given ownership, it was converted to use as a hospital and rest camp by the British Navy in 1728. Although the Navy left the island in 1733, the name survived until Errol Flynn purchased it in 1940. Falling in love with the area, he decided to convert it into his own personal Garden of Eden. Planting royal and coconut palms, he imported exotic birds like peacocks and parrots. After Flynn's death the island was sold and resold until it was purchased by California publishing magnate Harry Eiler. The island has three modest beaches. The one in front of the dock is the center for water sports. Crusoe's Beach is set off to one side, and small and sedate Trembly Knee Cove is clothing-optional. The island is also a great place for birdwatching, with white owls, peregrine hawks, and white egrets in residence. The Orchid Terrace and H.M.S. Bounty Bar has a room devoted to Errol Flynn memorabilia and screens his films on its VCR. A day's guest membership is just J$10 which covers the boat and is deductible from any purchase of J$35 or more. Personal food and beverages are prohibited. The ferry operates from 7 and ends at 1 AM with transport by request after that time.

PRACTICALITIES

accommodations: Admiralty Club on Navy Island has the most unusual accommodations in the area. There are 10 rooms available including seven studio bungalows and five bungalow suites. All have ceiling fans, louvered walls and doors, mosquito nets, balconies/verandas, small refrigerators. Studios are equipped with hot plates and some suites have kitchenettes. The suites are detached for privacy and have names like "Firefly." Activities include Errol Flynn movies screened on VCR, a weekly beach party, and backgammon and checker boards. Other famous resorts in the area include the exclusive Trident, Marbella Club at Dragon Bay, San San, and the Frenchman's Cove Hotel. See chart for more information.

budget accommodations: The most reasonably priced place listed by the tourist board is the De Montevin Guest House. Housed in a Victorian Gingerbread structure, it is one of the island's best known guesthouses. (See chart). Down the street are the Rose and Sunnyside guesthouses. Around the corner is the Scotia. Ivanhoe's (tel. 993-2681) is around the corner and down the street from Scotia. Next to the ruins of "The Reef" is the Little Reef Guest House at 1 Queen St. If you want to stay out on the east coast, it's best to ask around. One possibility in Long Bay is offered by Mr. B. J. "Kris" Kristensen (tel. 993-3678), a full-blooded Dane who has a four-bedroom cottage for rent at a very reasonable rate. Write Box 166, Port Antonio for full details. Also try Corinthis Vacation Cottage (tel. 993-3768).

dining out: Besides the Admiralty Club's Orchid Terrace on Navy Island, Mirabella and Frenchman's Cove also provide moderate to expensive dining. The expensive and super gourmet Trident has the most formal atmosphere. The De Montevin has Jamaican cuisine as does the restaurant right on the edge of the Blue Lagoon which features seafood.

budget dining: There are a number of restaurants in town. Try the Try Me on West St. Kingsley's, near the market, has local breakfast including the dreaded boiled bananas; they also have local food and slices of cake. Golden Happiness, across from the courthouse, has a large selection of reasonably priced Chinese food. They also have an attached a/c dining room. Atlantis Restaurant serves local cuisine; all entrees come with a cup of meat soup. The Ice Cream Parlour and Snack next to the Delmar Theatre features friendly local atmosphere and cuisine. The Sunnyside also has a restaurant. Box lunches are sold from a van weekdays around noon in front of Titchfield School. Stop Brap, at the edge of town on the way to Folly Estate, has jerk chicken and roast fish. Also try Centre Point out the same way. Coronation Bakery is one stop for your baked goods. Cool Runnins at 20 West St. has ice cream. Short Stop Mini Mart, R & R Supermarket, and Sang Hing Supermarket are on West St., Musgrave Market has the usual market scene featuring somnolent higglers. See the ven-

PORT ANTONIO ACCOMMODATIONS

KEY: S = Single; D = Double; 3rd = Third person sharing; S1 = 10% service charge; BA = Private bath/shower; P = Pool; B = Beach on property or in vicinity; EP = European Plan (no meals); CP = Continental Plan (breakfast included); FAP = Full American Plan (all meals included); AI = All inclusive

NOTE: Rates (in US$) are given as a guideline only; price fluctuations can and will occur. Summer season generally runs 4/15–11/15 or 12/15; check with hotel concerned for specifics. Hotel tax is levied on each room regardless of the number of people staying in it.

ADDRESS/ TELEPHONE	WINTER			SUMMER				NOTES
	S	D	ROOM TAX	S	D	ROOM TAX	# OF ROOMS	
Bonnie View Plantation Hotel, Box 82, Port Antonio (Richmond Hill), 993-2752/2862	40–44	60–65	4	34	51	2	20	S1, BA, P, EP
De Montevin Lodge, Box 85, Port Antonio (21 Fort George St.), 993-2604	23–25	36–40	4	17	34	2	13	S1, BA, B, EP
Faith Cottage, Box 50, Port Antonio (Dolphin Bay), 993-3703	75	110		60	90		8	BA, P, B, EP
Fern Hill Club, Port Antonio, 993-3243	Inquire			Inquire				BA, P, B
Frenchman's Cove Hotel, Port Antonio, 993-3224	Inquire			Inquire				BA, P, B
Goblin Hill Villas, Port Antonio, 925-8108	Inquire			Inquire				BA, P, B
Jamaica Palace Hotel, Box 277, Port Antonio, 993-2020	Inquire			Inquire				S1, BA, P, B, EP
Marbella Club at Dragon Bay, Port Antonio, 993-3281/3	Inquire			Inquire			100	BA, B, EP
Trident Villas and Hotel, Box 119, Port Antonio, 993-2602	250–350	300–530	12	110–150	130–330	8	26	BA, P, B, EP

dor who goes through holding a popsicle and violently enunci-
ating "POPsicle, POP." If you get out to Buff Bay, try Paceset-
ter's Cafeteria.

entertainment: Innumerable bars line the streets, but the
action's at City Club on West St., with canned reggae and
dancing every night. Inside, a line of Rastas, their locks fash-
ionably secured under large felt caps, move hands and beer
bottles up and down, jiving in time to the music. The Fern Hill
Club (tel. 993-3222) offers special events such as beach parties
and cultural shows. Also try Tunnel 54 Club at 54 Harbour St.
The sole movie theater, the Delmar, is on Harbour Street.

events: The Spring Marlin Tournament, held in the Marina,
takes place each April. The International Marlin Tournament,
one of the most prestigious sport fishing events in the Caribbean, is held at the Marina in October.

shopping: The main shops in town are the San Hing Gift
Shoppe in the City Centre Plaza and "The Oasis" down Harbour St. from the courthouse. The latter has books, jams,
woodwork, and tee shirts, Located next to the library, the
Town Talk Store proclaims itself "The Bargain Centre." Also
try Dijon, 4 Morris Ave., for clothes.

services: The Jamaica Tourist Board operates out of the second floor of City Centre Plaza. Banks include the Bank of
Commerce, 1 West St., and the Bank of Nova Scotia, 3 Harbour St.. Pharmacies include City Centre Pharmacy inside
City Centre Plaza and Square Deal at 11 West St.. The Admiralty Club (tel. 993–2667) at Navy Island has the most beautiful marina in the entire island. It offers Immigration and
Customs clearance, hot water showers, laundry and mail service, the full facilities of the resort, and other services. Write
Box 188, Port Antonio for full details. A number of car rental
agencies operate in town. For moped and bike rentals, visit
Stuart's at Tunnel Plaza. Scuba diver instructor Janet Lee
(993–3318) has her headquarters at San San Beach.

Port Antonio Harbour

Transport

getting around: It's easy to walk around the compact town. Take minibuses or buses from the square near the market to all outlying destinations or, if out of town, just stop whatever comes down the road.

tours: The Tiki Antonio (993–2667) offers sunset cruises which include a seven-course dinner. Daytime snorkeling and harbor cruises are also offered. One place to book raft trips is Rio Grande Attractions (tel. 993–2778).

from Port Antonio: Minibuses and buses leave from the area around the market for Ocho Rios, Moore Town and other destinations. Be aware that there are two routes to Kingston: one through Morant Bay and one via Buff Bay.

Moore Town and the John Crow Mountains

The area surrounding the Jim Crow Mountains and the Blue Mountains, which they abut, is one of the most picturesque in Jamaica. Unlike the side facing Kingston, the mountains here receive incredible amounts of rainfall and are virtually untouched. Lush and spectacular vegetation and views abound. As is the case in any area that has been populated for hundreds of years, the hills are alive with the sound of legends. The place names for gorges, creeks, mountain passes, and precipices each have a story to tell. And for hundreds of years now this area has been populated by the Windward Maroons, a people with their own special type of Maroon culture. See the "Cockpit Country" section to learn about Maroon history.

the Kromanti play: Jamaicans see the Maroons as possessing the most authentic African cultural tradition on the island. One substantiation for this is the "Kromanti Play" or "Kromanti Dance" which takes its name from the historical slaver depot situated along the coast of present-day Ghana. The Moore Town Maroons possess the richest and most varied Koromanti tradition. As in voodoo ceremonies elsewhere in Africa and the Americas, participants are possessed by ancestral spirits and take on their characteristics—even resorting to violence. The *fete man* ("fight man") presides over the ceremonies. He is a ritual doctor (known as a *myal*) who is expert in herbal and spiritual cures. The ceremonies themselves are directed towards healing injuries and psychological illnesses.

the ceremony: The Kromanti Play serves as a unifying and bonding force within the Maroon community. Participants gathered at the site pledge support to a common goal. The drumming begins with a lighthearted tone using styles like Jawbone, Saleone, and Tambu which combine "neo-African drumming" with European-influenced melodies and songs in English and Jamaicatalk. As the hours progress, the drumming gradually turns more serious and "deeper." Dancers form a ring or join in pairs and, as the intensity rises, the spirits feel the heart and join the beat—possessing the dancers. One man is possessed by the spirit of a dead *myal* who leaps into the center. The music turns more somber and sacred. Announcing one song after another, he is answered by the drums and leaps back and forth flailing a machete. He applies herbal remedies to the patient and runs through a series of ritualized motions as the drums and singing reek with tension. The ceremony peaks with the sacrifice of a fowl or hog.

musical roots: Modern day Maroon music and dance is like a map of Western Africa. The names themselves tell the story of retention of historical roots with Africa. And the more sacred and "deeper" Kromanti style names refer to the names historically given to African regions and ethnic groups from which the slaves come: "Mandinga" refers to Senegambian origin; "Mongola" is from Angola; Ibo refers to the Nigerian tribe of the same name; and Kromanti refers to the Gold Coast slaves. Despite the names, however, the drumming and dance styles have become so hybridized and influenced by each other that they have lost their ethnic specificity. The instruments, on the contrary, are the same as the ones currently in use in Africa and bear the same names. The Maroons have developed their own "drum language" similar to those currently used among the Akans of Ghana and the Ivory Coast. The "Kromanti Language" or "Country" spoken among Maroons in ceremonies is largely Akan derived. And the musical style combining both of these elements—songs with proverbs— resembles a similar tradition found among the Ashanti and Fanti peoples.

Moore Town: The home of the Windward Maroons, Moore Town lies on the eastern fork of the road running south from Port Antonio. Here, the local government consists of a Maroon colonel who—assisted by a Major, Captain, and Secretary— presides over a committee of 24 elected members. Village meetings take place on the common or recreation ground known as *Osofu* (meeting place).

Fronted by a graveyard, the Anglican Church, oldest building in town, is to the left as you enter. Across from the school, Bump Grave contains the remains of the national heroine Nanny, a Maroon leader who was a legendary fighter. Note the Maroon flag flying next to the Jamaican. Another Maroon settlement, Cornwall Barracks lies at the end of the same road. Cross the swinging rope bridge to visit Jupiter Falls next to a cave and mineral spring. Following the western fork of the road past colorfully-named Alligator Church, Ginger House, Comfort Castle, and Millbank, you reach Bowden's Pen, the rainiest spot in all Jamaica. rainfall of 1,259 cm (459 in.) was recorded here in 1959-60. A footpath leads over the mountains to Bath.

Nanny Town: Legendary, semimythical ruins of a Maroon settlement located to the southwest of Moore Town. British soldiers searched for over six years to find this stronghold. When they found it, Nanny, an 18th-C. guerrilla chieftainess, dumped vats of boiling water onto the troops from the heights above the town. After repeated attacks, the town was destroyed in 1734. Once it had been reclaimed by the jungle, a series of legends grew up around it. One maintains that none but a Maroon could go there and return alive. Another says that the white birds that fly out of the trees there are the *duppies* of Maroon warriors. In 1899, Police Inspector Hubert Thomas, asked by his superior officer to explore the place for any relics which might be of interest at the Jamaican exhibition to be held in Kingston the following year, was informed that Nanny was the wife of Cudjoe, the Maroon leader in the west part of the island. In May of 1890, investigating the site, he and members of the rural police force could find only one ancient bottle. Archaeological excavations were carried out here in 1973-74.

BATH

A small farming community, Bath is noted for its hotsprings and Botanical Garden. Officially named The Bath of St. Thomas the Apostle, the spring was discovered by a runaway slave in the 1690s. Discovering that the warm waters of a forest pool cured tropical ulcers on his legs, he returned to tell his owner about his miraculous discovery. The government bought the spring in 1699, and a town was promoted by a public corporation. Soon it became the most fashionable spot on the island. Political clashes during the late 1600s caused Bath to lose its fashionable image; it soon became a ghost town with only 10 inhabitants. Today, only the baths and the Botanical Gardens remain to attest to its former glory. The springs are unique because the water issues both hot and cold. The water, high in lime and sulfur, is regarded as being especially valuable in treating skin diseases and rheumatic ailments. Buy a ticket and bathe in one of the tanks inside the hotel, or take a hike up behind the hotel and bathe in the water flowing from an overhead bamboo pipe. While the hotel is set back at the end of a road leading from town, the Botanical Gardens are right in the center of town. Now a mere shadow of their former splendor, these are the second oldest gardens in the Western Hemisphere. Many of the plants and trees first introduced to Jamaica were planted here, including the original breadfruit trees brought over by Caption Bligh. The descendants of these trees may still be seen in one corner of the garden.

accommodations and food: Bath Fountain Hotel (tel. 982-2632/2315) has rooms. Use of the bath is included in the price. Although it's a bit rundown and deteriorating, it still retains its own special charm. The restaurant features Jamaican cuisine. As the hotel was badly damaged during 1988's Hurricane Gilbert, check and see if it's reopened if arriving without a reservation. There's also a small restaurant in the town itself. Avoid this hotel on weekends when Kingstonites arrive in hordes.

from Bath: A path leads over the Blue Mountains from Hayfield to Bowden Pen. Most frequent transport is to and from

Morant Bay. Transport to Hordley near the east coast is available but very infrequent. Count on walking unless you get lucky and hitch a ride.

MORANT BAY

Capital of St. Thomas Parish, this tiny town is of note chiefly for its historic associations with the Morant Bay Rebellion, which took place in 1865, led by Baptist deacon Paul Bogle. When Bogle along with 400 followers marched on Morant Bay Court House on 11 October to present their grievances, they clashed with the local volunteer militia. During the ensuing melee, the courthouse, seen as a symbol of injustice, was burned to the ground and many prominent citizens were murdered. Declaring martial law, the governor unleashed the soldiers on the local populace. Soldiers torched 1,000 homes and executed after courtsmartial more than 430 women and men. Using the uprising as an excuse to rid himself of a vociferous spokesman for the poor in the legislature, the governor had George Gordon brought to Morant Bay and, after framing him with responsibility for the uprising, ordered him hung in front of the charred ruins of the courthouse. Bogle suffered the same fate. As an aftermath of the controversy surrounding the handling of the uprising, the governor was recalled and Jamaica became a Crown Colony. The powerful and dynamic statue of Paul Bogle, sculpted by Edna Manley, stands in front of the rebuilt courthouse. During excavations in 1975, a total of 79 skeletons were found inside old refuse dumps located inside Morant Bay Fort.

vicinity of Morant Bay: Yallahs Ponds, nearby to the south of the highway, have twice the salinity of seawater due to evaporation. The early settlers obtained their salt here. The ruins of a small stone signal tower found here are listed as a National Monument. Judgment Cliff is a 1,600-m (1,000-ft.) escarpment visible from the Yallahs River. This is the only

Small boy, Bath

tangible reminder of the 1692 earthquake which sank Port Royal. According to local legend, it received its name when the landslide buried the plantation of a Dutchman who maltreated his slaves. Best view is from Easington. Cane River Falls can be reached from Bull Bay. Heading east along A4 from Morant Bay are the once-busy banana and sugar ports of Port Morant and Bowden. At one time guarded by Fort Lindsay on one side and Fort William on the other, Point Morant still has two fine beaches: Lyssons and Roselle. Between Bowden and the sea lies a low flat triangle of land known as Holland. Said to have been the most prosperous sugar plantation in Jamaica, it was owned by Simon Taylor, the wealthiest man in the W. Indies in his day. Just off the highway near Golden Grove lie the remains of Stokes Hall, one of the oldest holdings in Jamaica. Morant Bay Lighthouse is set between Quaco and South East Point.

KINGSTON

INTRODUCTION

A city of contrasts, Kingston is the capital and also the largest (pop. 850,000) English-speaking city south of Miami. Not only is the island's most expensive architecture found here, but the worst poverty as well. Old Georgian buldings and soaring sky-scrapers contrast vividly with the JLP and PNP graffiti that demarcate political zones in Kingston's turbulent slums. "Kings-town hot-to" goes the reggae song, implying the city's underlying social stresses. In this economically and politically polarized city, tension lies pulsating just under the surface. Sometimes it explodes and results in shootings and gang wars in W. Kingston. Kingston, however, is a much safer city to visit than New York or Miami. From the harbor, Kingston spreads out across the fan-shaped Liguanea Plains to the first slopes of the Blue Mountains. Downtown Kingston is a quiet collection of streets which still retain a bit of charm. New Kingston, a plastic city-within-a-city containing the edifices of the multinationals and banks, is the hub of business operations in Jamaica. Halfway Tree and Cross Roads are the major reference and transportation transfer points.

history: Kingston started out as Colonel Barry's Hog Crawle in the 1600s. After Port Royal was devastated during the 1692 earthquake, survivors flocked to Kingston. Land was purchased, and the streets were laid out on a grid pattern which remains intact to this day. In 1802 Kingston was chartered as a Corporation with Mayor and Council; it became the capital in 1872. The 1907 earthquake and fire destroyed many of the

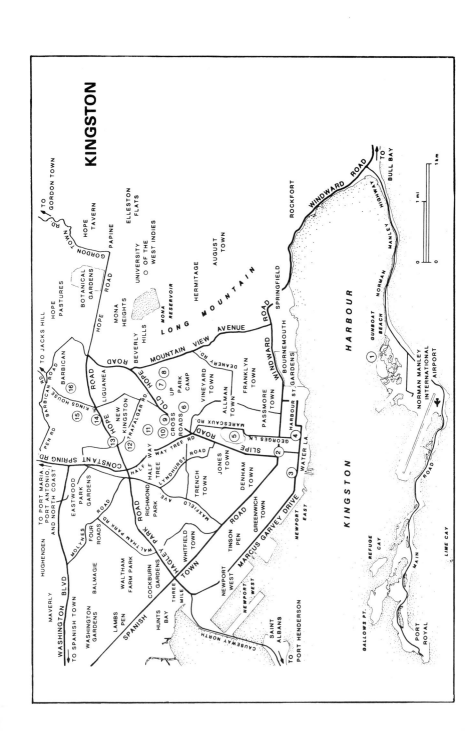

KINGSTON

old buildings downtown. Since 1960, a major effort has been underway to revitalize this area through renovation and construction.

getting there: Minibuses run regularly from Montego Bay, Ocho Rios, Mandeville, and Port Antonio. Trans Jamaican flies here from Montego Bay, Ocho Rios, and Port Antonio. There's also slow but inexpensive train service between Montego Bay, Williamsfield (Mandeville), and Kingston.

arriving by air: Norman Manley Airport has all the charm and grace of a Greyhound bus terminal *sans* winos. It does feature a small snack bar, another in the "waving gallery"—in which one seldom or never sees anyone waving—and a somewhat formal restaurant. If you're intent on grabbing a last-minute souvenir for some casual acquaintance you've nearly forgotten about, Bookland has a number of postcards, semi-tacky souvenirs, and Jamaican-made perfumes with fragrances like "Khus Khus." But the place to go is the post office where philatelic commemoratives are sold along with J$2 tokens to the UCC coffee machine. All proceeds are donated by Japanese-owned UCC Blue Mountain to the S.O.S. Village, an orphan's home in Stony Hill. Here's your chance to be charitable and buy an inexpensive souvenir of two countries while having only been to one of them. If you're not a canned coffee buff, you can pick up an ice cold can of Ramunade (sic) which contains "flavour, sugar water, and L Ascorbic acid." The airport's most interesting sight is Carl Abraham's mural of Ja-

---

KINGSTON AND
LOWER ST. ANDREW

1. Palisadoes Park
2. Parade
3. Railway Station
4. National Gallery
5. National Heroes Park
6. Little Theater and Public Archives
7. National Arena
8. National Stadium

9. USIS
10. Pegasus Hotel
11. Jamaica Tourist Board
12. Mrs. Johnson
13. Devon House
14. Jamaica House
15. Kings House
16. Sandhurst

maican life on the wall down from the coffee house. Taxis leave out front. Buses leave from the airport at regular intervals. Buses to Port Royal pass by the roundabout, but they are rare.

SIGHTS

downtown: The newly revitalized Parade has a bandstand for concerts and an amphitheater for dramatic presentations. A series of fountains is divided into four pools. The fountains are lit at night with multicolored lamps. Its history dates back to the 18th C. when it housed military barracks prior to their removal to Up Park Camp in the mid-1800s. Military parades of soldiers were conducted on the grounds. It was opened to the public in 1872 when Kingston became the capital. Higglers have been confined to an area at the east where a riotous cacophony of goods are displayed. Anything can happen within the Parade and on surrounding streets. You might see a female

Sidney McLaren, Parade *(1979)*

Revival Zion group playing African drums and singing. Sound systems blare upon streets, playing the current bass-orientated "downpression" music that passes for reggae these days. On the sidewalks of nearby streets, males dance as though in a hypnotic trance. On one side of the Parade is Kingston Parish Church. Reconstructed in 1909, the current building is modeled after the original which was destroyed in the 1907 earthquake. The Ward Theatre stands on a site which has been used continually for drama performances over centuries. Built in 1911, and open every year from 26 Dec. (Boxing day) until April or May, it's home to the annual Panto-mime, a national institution. Duke Street contains some note-worthy buildings, including the island's only Jewish Synagogue (The United Congregation of Israelites), St. An-drew Scots Kirk Church, and Gordon House, home of Jamai-ca's Parliament. Facing Gordon House is Headquarters House, one of the most historic buildings in Jamaica. Originally named Hibbert House after the man who built it, the name was changed after it became military headquarters in 1814 for the resident British military commander. It was constructed after Thomas Hibbert bet three other merchants in the 1750s to see who could build the finest and most elegant house. Of the four homes built, only Headquarters House remains stand-ing. In 1872 it became the office of the Colonial Secretary and the meeting place for Jamaica's legislature. After the legisla-ture moved to Gordon House in 1960, Headquarters House re-mained vacant until the Jamaica National Trust Commission moved its headquarters here in 1983. Vale Royal, on Montrose Rd., is the prime minister's residence. The house, which has been in continuous use as a residence since the late 17th C., has a lookout tower on the roof which was used to keep track of the movement of ships in the harbor. National Heroes Park, along the way to Cross Roads, has modern monuments dedi-cated to national heroes George William Gordon and Paul Bo-gle, as well as the tombs of Marcus Garvey, Alexander Bustamante, and Norman Manley.

museums: The National Art Gallery, Kingston Mall, located in the Roy West Building at the corner of Ocean Blvd. and Orange St., has one of the most outstanding collections in the

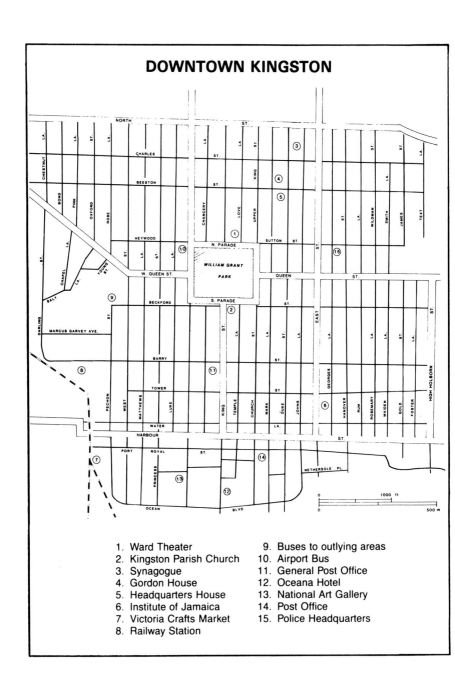

DOWNTOWN KINGSTON

1. Ward Theater
2. Kingston Parish Church
3. Synagogue
4. Gordon House
5. Headquarters House
6. Institute of Jamaica
7. Victoria Crafts Market
8. Railway Station
9. Buses to outlying areas
10. Airport Bus
11. General Post Office
12. Oceana Hotel
13. National Art Gallery
14. Post Office
15. Police Headquarters

Caribbean (open Mon. to Sat., 10-5, J$1 suggested contribu-
tion). The ground floor is dominated by Christopher Gonzales'
gigantic bronze of Bob Marley; the upstairs is divided into
chronological periods beginning with early Intuitives like
John Dunkley and David Miller. Also included is nearly everything Edna Manley ever sculpted, works by Carl Abrahams
and Karl Parboosingh, stellar fantasies by Tina Matkovic and
Colin Garland, and artwork by later Intuitives like Sidney Mc-
Laren. One entire room is packed with the products of the
presiding genius of Jamaican art, Kapo (Mallica Reynolds).
The Annual National Exhibiton, featuring works by the island's best artists, is held here from Dec. through February. At
its headquarters on East St., the Institute of Jamaica (Mon. to
Fri., 9-5) has a small Natural History Museum; special exhibits are held on the floor above it. In 1986 the Bob Marley
Museum opened at 56 Hope Road. Its highlight is the mural
"The Journey of Bob Marley Superstar" by Everald Brown.
Other features include a Marley video, a wax statue, and a
painted statue out front of Bob kicking a soccer ball. The Coin
and Note Museum is in the Bank of Jamaica building along
the waterfront. Forces Museum, containing military memorabilia, is on Up Camp Road.

Devon House and vicinity: On Hope Rd. past Halfway
Tree. Gleeming white and attractively landscaped, this stunning example of Georgian architecture has been restored by
the National Trust. George Stiebel, the first black millionaire
in the Caribbean, built this three-story house in 1881. Shops
on the grounds surrounding the house sell pricey goods to foreigners and rich Jamaicans. Although the grounds are open
daily, most of the shops are closed on Sun. and Mon.

Farther north modern Jamaica House was the prime minister's residence for a short period after its construction until it
was converted into his office. Farther still is King's House.
Official residence of the governor general, it was originally the
home of the bishop of Jamaica. It was rebuilt two years after
being wrecked in the 1907 earthquake. Open to visitors weekdays 9-5, it is set amidst 200 expertly landscaped acres.

Devon House

Hope Botanical Garden and Zoo: On 200 acres of land on
the north side of Old Hope Rd., these gardens were laid out in
1881 after the government acquired the land from the Hope
Estate. Originally an experimental garden, they were transformed into the Royal Botanical Gardens for the occasion of
Queen Elizabeth's 1953 visit. In addition to the orchid house,
there are Indonesian sago palms, a small zoo, a children's
amusement park, and a stone aqueduct (open daily 8-6).

University of the West Indies: Located along Mona Rd. in
E. Kingston, this attractive campus has a unique history.
Originally the site of the Mona Sugar Estate, there are ruins
of mills, aqueducts, and a now silent water wheel. The original
wooden buildings here were used as a center for Jewish refu-
gees during WWII. The Chapel, located near the main entrance, was originally a sugar warehouse at Gales Valley
Estate in Trelawny before it was dismantled stone-by-stone
and reassembled here. Note that the original owner's name
and date of construction can be seen along the top of the pedi-

King's House

ment just under the roof. The crests of the members of this international university are set inside the chapel.

PRACTICALITIES

accommodations: Chief draw downtown is the Oceana with 200 rooms. Conveniently located right on the harbor, the hotel is just a short walk from the National Gallery and the Parade. It has a pool and an attached conference center equipped with eight meeting and banquet rooms for groups of up to 1,200.

Ample presentation equipment is available for use. For those who need a yet larger space, the adjoining Jamaica Conference Centre ranks with the finest worldwide. The largest of its five rooms holds 1,050 persons and features an electronic voting system. Other major hotels include the Jamaica Pegasus, the Sandhurst, The Courtleigh, Wyndham Hotel, and Terra Nova Hotel. (See charts for rates and information).

budget accommodations: Mrs. Johnson (tel. 926-0296) runs the city's pre-eminent bed and breakfast. Located at 2 Holburn Rd. next to the Indies Hotel, this high spirited and hospitable lady charges around US$12 pp pn which includes a simple fried egg and toast breakfast. The rooms are cleaned daily, and there are private showers. A TV resides in the foyer. If Mrs. Johnson is full, try Mrs. Perry down the street. The following hotels are not listed by the Tourist Board. Altamont Court (tel. 929-4497-8), 1 Altamont Crescent, Kingston 5 has a/c rooms plus a swimming pool. The Chelsea Hotel, Chelsea Ave., New Kingston, has a J$160 rate for foreigners. Danesbury Guest House (tel. 926-5178) is at 5 Ivy Green Crescent, Kingston 5. The International Inn, Derrymore Rd. Kingston 10, is a restaurant bar which rents rooms. Mountain Valley Hotel (tel. 924-2313) is on Old Stony Hill Rd., Kingston 8.

dining out: Fort Charles Restaurant is inside the Oceana. The El Dorado inside the Terra Nova restaurant has fixed price business lunches and a seafood buffet on Fridays. Rumours is at 3 Dumfries Road. One popular spot is the Orchid, 3 Waterloo Ave., which—naturally enough—has a lot of orchids on the property. Try the Talk of the Town with a commanding view and the less expensive Surrey Tavern in the Jamaica Pegasus. Also top floor and top price, the Ristorante d'Amour sits atop the Wyndham. The Hotel Four Seasons is at 18 Ruthven Road. The Hot Pot, 2 Altamont Terrace in New Kingston, caters to yuppies. Pirate's Seafood Restaurant and Rooftop Bar is opposite the Oceana. Norma, Belmont Rd., is yet another gourmet restaurant. Located at Devon House in what was once the carriage house and stables, The Grogge Shop specializes in Jamaican cuisine. Managed by Guyanans, Kohinoor Restaurant, 11 Ruthven Rd., serves main courses for J$20-45. Man-

KINGSTON ACCOMMODATIONS

KEY: S = Single; D = Double; 3rd = Third person sharing; S1 = 10% service charge; S3 = 5% service charge; S4 = 12 1/2% service charge; S5 = 12% service charge; BA = Private bath/shower; P = Pool; B = Beach on property or in vicinity; EP = European Plan (no meals); CP = Continental Plan (breakfast included); FAP = Full American Plan (all meals included); AI = All inclusive

NOTE: Rates (in US$) are given as a guideline only; price fluctuations can and will occur. Summer season generally runs 4/15–11/15 or 12/15; check with hotel concerned for specifics. Hotel tax is levied on each room regardless of the number of people staying in it.

ADDRESS/ TELEPHONE	WINTER S	D	ROOM TAX	SUMMER S	D	ROOM TAX	# OF ROOMS	NOTES
The Courtleigh, 31 Trafalgar Road, Kingston 10, 926-8174, 929-5320/4	48.50–70	55–70	8	48.50–65	55–65	6	72	S1, BA, E, EP
Hotel Four Seasons, Box 190, Kingston 10 (18 Ruthven Road), 926-6805/0682, 929-7655	50	50–55	8	50	50–55	4	39	S1, BA, EP
Indies Hotel, 5 Hoburn Road, Kingston 10, 926-2952/0989	Inquire		4	Inquire		2	14	S3, BA, EP
Ivor Guest House, Jack's Hill P.A., St. Andrew, 927-1460	Inquire			40	60		4	S5, BA, CP
Jamaica Pegasus, Box 333, Kingston 5 (81 Knutsford Blvd.), 926-3690/9	Inquire		8	130–145	130–145	12	350	S4, BA, P, EP
Mayfair Hotel, Box 163, Kingston 10 (4 West King's House Close), 926-1610	35–40	40–50	8	35–45	40–50	4	30	S1, BA, P, EP
Medallion Hall, 53 Hope Road, Kingston 6, 927-5721/5866	53	58	4	55–65	55–65	2	13	S1, BA, EP

Kingston Accommodations (*continued*)

	WINTER			SUMMER				
Morgan's Harbour Hotel, Port Royal, Kingston 1, 924-8562	Inquire		4	75	90	2	27	S1, BA, P, B, EP
Oceana Hotel and Conference Center, Box 986, Kingston (2 King St.), 922-0920/9	70–80		10	80–100		6	200	S1, BA, P, EP
Pine Grove, Content Gap, St. Andrew, 922-8705	38–75	45–77	4	38–45	45–56	6	15	S1, BA, EP
Sandhurst, 70 Sandhurst Cres., Kingston 6, 927-7239/8244	28–34	36–44	4	28–34	36–44	2	35	S1, BA, P, EP
Sutton Place Hotel, 11 Ruthven Road, Kingston 10, 926-1207/2297	40–70		8	40–70		4	33	BA, P, EP
Terra Nova Hotel, 17 Waterloo Road, Kingston 10, 926-2211/9334	70–85		10	70		6	28	S1, BA, P, EP
Tropical Inn, 19 Clieveden Ave., Kingston 6, 927-9917/8, 927-9931	Inquire			45–90	55	2	24	S1, BA, P, EP
Wyndham Hotel, 77 Knutsford Blvd., Kingston 5, 926-5430	95–105		12	105–135		8	400	S1, BA, P, EP

tana's Restaurant, 2 1/4 Ruthven Rd., serves Jamaica dishes for J$25 and up. Shish Kebab, Holburn Rd., specializes in Lebanese cuisine. For Chinese food, try the Village Plaza on Constant Springs Road, the Golden Dragon on Mona Plaza, or the Lychee Garden inside New Kingston Mall. Approachable by limousine from some of the major hotels, the Blue Mountain Inn sits inside a great house on a former coffee plantation. The Arms is out at historic Port Henderson.

budget dining: In the new Kingston area many carts serve box lunches to go. There are a wide variety of lunchrooms on

the second storey of New Kingston Mall. Inside Spanish Court
Plaza, Gino's Fast Food has reasonable prices. FRENZ at Half
Way Tree stocks fast food, ice cream, pastries, and beverages.
Other fast food restaurants at Half Way Tree include Mother's,
Uncle Sam's (open 24 hours), and Fireside Fast Food. Infamous
for its transformation of Central American rainforests into
grazing pasture for cattle, Burger King is a landmark on the
Half Way Tree landscape. Its J$12 Whopper really packs them
in. It's also the only place open on Sunday mornings for breakfast. Baked in split, hinged oil barrels on legs, BBQ chicken
legs are sold on the street at Half Way Tree, as are fish
wrapped in foil. Rastafarian *ital* (vegetarian) restaurants include the Ethiopia and Mimi's Ethiopian Herbal on Old Hope
Rd. Open air, comfortable, and moderately priced, Peppers, at
Annette Crescent and Upper Waterloo Rd., caters to a mostly
middle class crowd; it serves jerk chicken, pork, and fish. Chelsea Jerk Centre, Chelsea Ave., New Kingston, has jerk pork
and chicken with a fish tea and roast fish stand. Try Sugar
and Spice, 131 Old Hope Rd. for patties, cheesecake, and other
treats. At Devon House, "I Scream" offers cups, cones, and
shakes in a variety of flavors including rum and raisin, and
the Brick Oven features baked goods. If you're looking for
something that packs a punch, the Grogge Shoppe's fancy rum
drinks are acclaimed. Montano Supermarket is on Hope Rd.
at Half Way Tree. The amazing edifice that constitutes John
R. Wong's Supermarket lies perpendicular to Spanish Court
Plaza on Trafalgar Rd. Inside, a red digital readout placard
pours out a stream of customary platitudes about service and
the like and warns shoplifters that they "will be arrested and
prosecuted to the full extent of the law." Homepride Bakery &
Sandwich Shop is inside. Sample food prices: J$10.50 per doz.
eggs, J$10.89 per lb. butter, J$19.33 for 1.9 litres of OJ, J$5 for
a can of soup, J$42.75 for 8 oz. of Blue Mountain coffee beans,
J$19 for 26 oz. of honey, J$12.50 per bottle of roots wine,
J$21.25 for 32 oz. of corn oil, J$13.45 for 3 fl. oz. of Listerine,
J$22 of a 4-pack of Duracell AA alkaline batteries, J$9.50 per
lb. for tomatoes, and J$6.50 per lb. for carrots. To pick up
American goods like peanut butter and Kellogg's cornflakes,
visit the Small Business Association Flea Market held every
Sunday at the Randy Williams Entertainment Centre on Hope

Rd. next to Jamaica House. You might run into Mutabaruka here.

downtown budget dining: Good value for the money and atmosphere, The Bracera is set on the second floor of the Convention Centre at the end of Duke St. It features cafeteria-style food (with table service available for an additional J$20 charge), swirling ceiling fans, and overhead woven rattan baskets set into a yellow ochre egg carton grid. The wonderfully cacophonous Duke's, corner Duke and Queen Sts., has tasty local cuisine. Purchase tickets at the wire mesh window, hand them over at the door to the kitchen, and take a seat in the partitioned dining area. Act II, a cafeteria, is at Duke and Harbour Sts. Above Colonel Sanders, Kentucky Fried Chicken, Port Royal and King Sts., a Colonel Sanders flag battles for supremacy with the Jamaican colors. Try their biscuits. For traditional drinks like Irish Moss and Pepup (agar, peanuts, oats, condensed milk, and spices), visit Morales Juice Counter at 46 Church St. and Cynth's at 96 Church St.

entertainment: The Ward Theater on the Parade is the best place on the island to hear music and view dramatic performances. Artists like the national Dance Theater Company, L'Acadco, and Olive Lewin's Jamaica Folk Singers regularly perform here. It features a year-round schedule with very reasonable ticket prices. If you're sitting in the balcony, you may notice the plush red seats in the center: they're reserved for dignitaries like the Governor General. The Little Theater, Tom Redcam Drive, also features a wide range of entertainment, and the Green Gables Theatre, Cargill Rd., presents plays. The Terra Nova Hotel, 17 Waterloo Rd., stages a number of events. The U.W.I. Creative Arts Center inside the University at Mona presents student performances. Live concerts are also occasionally held at the Oceana, the National Stadium, and Randy Williams Performance Centre. For jazz, visit the Surrey Tavern of the Pegasus on Tues. and Thurs. nights and the basement of the Mutual Life Building on Oxford Rd. on the last Wed. of every month beginning at 8 PM. Movie theaters include the Odeon at Half Way Tree, Carib at Cross Roads, and the Drive In (which also has seats!) off Holburn Rd. Located at 7 1/2 Constant Spring Road in the heart of Half Way Tree, Skateland Rolla Disco is undoubtedly the only club of its kind in all of the world. Created in 1969 by owner and manager Clinton (Jingles) Davy, it presents a once-in-a-lifetime opportunity to roller skate to reggae. Pennants are suspended overhead, and skaters—young and old alike—move back and forth along the huge rink in time to the reggae riddims. Its walls are decorated with colorful pictures, notices, and slogans. One declares "Skate carefully for your assurance. We carry no insurance." Popeye holds a "No smokin ganja ya" sign. Others declare "If you don't love children, don't even enter," and "Through These Gates Pass The Most Talented People on Earth." You might see any thing in here from a couple skating in tandem to a dread wearing a ski cap with Ethiopian colors dancing alone to the side. In the rear to the right, portable metal bookcases filled with an assortment of turntables, tape decks, and amps, stand next to piles and piles of albums and 45s. Skates are for rent above and beyond the modest admission fee, and there's a live band every Wednesday night. For quite a different scene try Mantana's Restaurant, 2 1/4 Ruthven, where middle-aged housewives accompanying pert hubbies gaze on stolidly as a pudgy go go dancer goes through the motions. The Rock Club at Meadowbrook features a mix of reggae, disco, and soca music and an 18-to-40 crowd. Swiss-owned The Club, Knutsford Blvd., New Kingston, plays reggae and disco for 17-to-25 year olds. The Epiphany (J\$25 pp with dress restrictions) is at Spanish Court, New Kingston. Illusions, in New South Plaza at 2 South Ave. near Constant Spring Rd., caters to the elite as does Mingles at the Courtleigh in New Kingston. Sweat is inside the Old Spanish Town Bar. Older folks congregate at the Jonkanoo Lounge at the Wyndham Hotel. The Oceana, downtown at 2 King St., features the Mutiny Disco. Also try the Odyssey and Seawitch on Knutsford Blvd. and Tit-for-Tat and Turntable Club on Red Hills Rd. The Student Union at the University of the West Indies has a bar and disco. The best and cheapest form of entertainment may be roaming around Half Way Tree, taking in the sights and watching the "crown and ankle"(Jamaican card and dice) games. Hookers stalk Trafalgar Road.

events: The UWI Carnival is held in February at the University of the West Indies at Mona. Cricket games take place in Sabina Park. A trade exhibition is held in March every other year at the National Arena. Her Excellency's May Day Charities, comprising a buffet supper, music and dance, and a fashion show, happens on the grounds of Kings House in May. In the same month, the largest flower show in the Caribbean, the Jamaica Horticultural Society Show, is held at the National Arena. An annual Ikebana International show is in June. At the end of June, the All Jamaica/ J. L. T. A. Circuit Open/Pro Championship takes place at the Jamaica Lawn Tennis Association Headquarters. Many events centering around the Independence Festival are held in Kingston in July. These include the finals of the National Festival Song Competition, held at the National Arena, and the finals of the Annual Gospel Song Festival at the Randy Williams Entertainment Centre. A "mini carnival" in celebration of U.S. Independence Day, happens at 6 Bamboo Avenue around July 4th. At the end of the month, the Mello-Go-Round, an annual presentation of the performing arts, is held at the National arena as is the Festival King & Queen Costume Show. The Jamaica Orchid Society's Fall Show takes place at the beginning of October. The Pirate's Race, which ends in Grand Cayman, begins from Port Royal in mid-October. The Annual International Show Jumping Extravaganza and Horse Trials is held at the Cayamanas Polo Grounds in November.

shopping: A variety of goods are available at the "duty free" stores in town. Some of the more famous shops for luxury items (cameras, china, crystal, watches, jewelry, perfume, etc.) include the Bijoux in New Kingston, K. Chandiram in the Pegasus, India House, 60 King St., The Carousel, 24 King St., and the Swiss Stores scattered about town. Also try Premier Plaza off Constant Spring Rd. near Half Way Tree and Spanish Court Plaza in New Kingston. Devon House also has a number of shops. At the Morales Health Food Store, 46 Church St., you can buy unique souvenirs like packets of dried sorrel, nerve powder, comfrey root, and "USE IT UP," a tonic with 31 herbs.

market shopping: The crafts market on the waterfront west of Victoria Pier (closed Sun.) is the local handicraft market which caters to visiting cruise ships and tourists. Coronation Market, a short walk from the Parade, provides a vivid, fascinating contrast with its down-to-earth, hustle-and-bustle atmosphere. Papine, a much smaller market located near the U. W. I. campus, has market days on Thurs. and Saturdays. A flea market takes place on Sun. at the Drive In Theater in New Kingston.

books and records: Kingston Bookshop Ltd. is at 70B King Street. Sangster's, the largest chain store, has branches at 33 King St., 97 Harbour St., 144 Old Hope Rd., and at 101 Water Lane. Times Store is at 8 King St., and Intellect Bookstore is at 20 Spanish Cresent. Books are also sold at the sales counter inside the Institute of Jamaica. Innumerable stores sell reggae albums. Try Randy's and Joe Gibb's on the Parade, any of the chain of Music Fare shops, or the African Museum at 2 Chancery Lane, N. Parade. Many shops are on Orange St., including Bunny Wailer's Cash and Carry, Augustus Pablo's, Tuff Gong, and Prince Buster. Music City is on E. Queen St. and Aquarius is on Halfway Tree Road. High Times in Kingston Mall has an exceptionally good selection. Discounts for quantity available at Sonic Sounds, Ritriment Road.

art galleries: Great places to window shop. Upstairs Downstairs, Harbour St., features some of Jamaica's most renowned artists. Frame Center is at Tangerine Place off Halfway Tree Road. Bolivar Gallery, corner Halfway Tree and Grove roads, also contains a small bookshop. Mutual Life Gallery, corner Oxford and Old Hope roads, has assorted works by local artists. Olympia Art Center is at the end of Old Hope Rd. near Papine.

services and information: The Jamaican Tourist Board (tel. 92-69280, 92-98070) is located in the New Kingston Office Complex, 77-83 Knutsford Blvd., next to the New Kingston Hotel in the heart of New Kingston (Mon. to Fri. 8:30–4:30). General information and pamphlets on Jamaica may be obtained from Jamaica Information Service, 58A Half Way Tree Road. Banks (only a small black market here) are centered in New Kingston. The General Post Office, which has a philatelic service, is on Temple Lane downtown (open Mon. to Thurs., 9-

5, Fri., 9-4, Sat., 9-1). Other major post offices are at Half Way Tree, Cross Roads, corner Barbican and Hope roads, Three Mile, and on Winward Rd. near Mountain View Road. Pay phones in downtown Kingston are scare. Try in front of the post office and inside Kingston Mall. There's a pricey laundromat next to the Chelsea Hotel, Chelsea Ave., New Kingston. Leslie Moodie Pharmacy is at 52A Church St.; Parade Pharmacy is at 21A West Parade; Arcade Pharmacy is at Church and Law Sts. Good service and local prices at Dixon Barbers, 116 Harbour St. at King St. To make reservations for the cabins in the Blue Mountains, contact the Forestry Dept. at 173 Constant Springs Rd. (tel. 42-667, 42-612). The U. S. Embassy is at 2 Oxford Rd., while the British High Commission is on Trafalgar Road. The German Embassy is at 10 Waterloo Rd., and the French Embassy is located at 60 Knutsford Boulevard. Immigration is at 230 Spanish Town Road. Take a bus from Half Way Tree to Three Miles before changing to a Spanish Town bus (open Mon. to Fri., 9-3).

libraries: National Library of Jamaica, located next door to the Institute of Jamaica on East St., has books and newspapers on file. It contains the largest collection of W. Indies material of any library in the world (open Mon. to Thurs., 9-5, Fri., 9-4, Sat., 9-1). Kingston and St. Andrew Parish Library is at 2 Tom Redcam Drive. The Afro Caribbean Institute (Mon. to Fri., 9-12), 11 Worth St., has a small library. United States Information Service (USIS: Mon. to Fri., 9-4) is on the first floor, Mutual Life Bldg., corner Oxford and Old Hope roads. The British High Commission (Mon. to Fri., 8:30-4:30), Trafalgar Rd., has a reading room. The Australian High Commission (Mon. to Thurs., 8-5, Fri., 8-12:30) has plenty of books from over, down and under.

sports and tours: The Adonis Health Club is below Pirate's Seafood Restaurant & Rooftop Bar on the promenade just down from the Oceana. Visitors may use the facilities of Constant Spring Golf Club (which includes golf course; tennis, badminton, and squash courts; and a pool) for a fee; temporary memberships are also available. To go on hikes in the Blue Mountains contact Peter Bentley (tel. 927-2097) at Maya Lodge and Hiking Center, Juba Spring, Peter's Rock Road, Jack's Hill. City and other tours are also available through Peter.

dealing with locals: Most Kingstonites are kind, courteous, and polite. You'll meet hustlers near your hotel and the airport. Just remember that no Jamaican in his right mind enters the slum areas. Sure, Bob Marley grew up in Trenchtown. But he got out.

Transport

getting around: After the heavily indebted city bus service was abandoned in 1984, routes were franchised out to privately owned minibuses. The bus system remains in a state of chaos. Amidst battalions of sky juice carts occupying the concrete passenger platforms, buses of every size, shape, and description leave from the Parade. It's best to ask a local which one to board. Take buses back and forth between the Parade and New Kingston (Half Way Tree). Within these two areas, you should be able to walk most places you'll need to go.

from Kingston: Bus service is available to just about any point on the island. With the exception of Spanish Town/ Mandeville buses which leave from Half Way Tree, most start from the vicinity of the Parade downtown. Ask around. The Ocho Rios Shuttle, operated by Econotours (tel. 24922, 27538), departs Kingston between 7:30 and 8 AM; it costs US$20 pp. Trains leave for Spanish Town, Williamsfield (Mandeville), and Montego Bay from Kingston's railway station located at the west end of Barry Street.
by air: Direct or connecting flights are available to virtually any N. American destination. Trans Jamaica also flies to Ocho Rios, Port Antonio, and Montego Bay.

VICINITY OF KINGSTON

Port Henderson

Situated across the bay from Port Royal. Can be reached by bus either from Spanish Town, or Kingston via Three Miles. Once a bustling and prosperous embarcation point for Spanish Town, today Port Henderson is reduced to a small village next to a shopping center. During the 18th C., while Spanish Town was still the island's capital, it was the chief point of arrival for visitors. It became a flourishing health and vacation resort during the 19th C. when its cold-water bathing pool was known as The Spa. As Spanish Town's fortunes waned so did those of Port Henderson. After The Spa disappeared in the 1951 hurricane, so did most of Port Henderson's income and population. Although it has been restored and preserved by the Jamaica National Trust Commission, it remains virtually unknown and unvisited—even by Jamaicans.

sights: The ruins of the Green Castle great house overlook the harbor, along with those of the smaller Bullock's Lodge just below. Fire has destroyed the restored Old Water Police Station, but the Longhouse remains intact. Used as an inn and lodging house until 1898, its name comes from its rectangular shape. The small, handsome building of dressed stone which once housed the public latrine now contains government offices. Eat at The Arms restaurant

Fort Clarence and Hellshire: Originally settled by Arawaks, this arid but spectacularly scenic area plays host to the island's last remaining iguanas and conies (Jamaica's only indigenous land mammal). Take a bus from Half Way Tree to Three Miles, then walk past Ziggy Records Manufacturing on the left until you reach the main road. Then take another bus to the right, get off at Fort Clarence roundabout and walk to Fort Clarence Beach (open Mon. to Fri., 10–5; Sat. to Sun., 9–5, free admission). Beautiful location, and almost exclusively a Jamaican crowd. Vendors are prohibited so there're no hassles.

Continue along the beach to the right to Half Moon Bay Fishing Authority. Many stands here sell fried fish and bammy, festival (delicious sweet fried bread), and drinking coconuts. Continue along to find a desolate cactus and coral headland area which stretches along the coast. Just you and the birds and the sea. Follow the main road farther down in the same direction to find many deserted white sand beaches with underground coves. Two Sisters Cave, in this area, has an Arawak-inscribed petroglyph of a human face. Be careful of currents while swimming.

Port Royal

Once known as the "City of Gold" and the "Babylon of the West," Port Royal is now an unimpressive fishing village, a mere shadow of its former self. Only a few historical sites remain to tell the tale of what was "the wickedest city in the world" when Kingston, across the bay, was still only the site of a hog corral.

getting there: Easiest way is to take the ferry (J$1) from the No. 1 Pier near the Victoria Crafts Market. (Departs Mon. to Fri. at 6, 7, 10, 12:30, 2:30, 5, 6:30; Sat. at 6, 6:30, 8, 8:30, 10, 10:30, 12:30, 1:15, 2, 2:30, 4:30, 5, 6:30, 7; Sun. at 11:30, 2:30, 4:30, 6:30.) Sit on the top deck, bask in the sun, and take in the view. Otherwise, take a bus from Kingston to the beginning of the Palisadoes (the 10-mile spit of land that contains Norman Manley Airport) and hitch.

history: Originally named Cayo de Carena (Careening Cay) by the Spaniards who discovered it, the English initially named it Cagway or The Point. Recognizing its strategic importance, the English built Fort Cromwell (later Fort Charles) within a year of their arrival. Eventually it was ringed by a network of six forts, stationing 2,500 men. Soon, a town sprang up to service the needs of the traders and buccaneers (a polite term for pirates). Encouraged by the government, the buccaneers used Port Royal as a base for their attacks upon

Fort Charles, Port Royal

Spanish ports as well as a place to dispose of their ill-gotten gains. As the buccaneers proliferated, so did the number of prostitutes and goldsmiths; the ratio of taverns and rum shops grew to one for every 10 residents. More than 2,000 buildings were jammed on this small cay, some erected on pilings driven into the sand. Rents soared to equal those of the poshest areas of London. A legend in his own time, Welsh adventurer Henry Morgan was the most colorful figure to emerge out of Port Royal. Within a few years, he carried out five daring, highly successful raids. His sacking of Panama in 1671, coming as it did after the signing of a peace treaty between Britain and Spain, caused him, along with his patron the governor, to be

brought back to London to stand trial. Although Gov. Mody-
ford was imprisoned in order to appease the Spaniards, Morgan was knighted and returned in triumph as Lt. Governor.
Another legendary figure of the same era, Britain's greatest
naval hero, Admiral Horatio Nelson, was twice stationed in
Port Royal.

earthquake of 1692: To many it seemed like divine retribu-
tion when this "City of Sin" was hit by a devastating earthquake and tidal wave on 7 June 1692. The tidal wave, which
followed the third shock, tossed one ship onto the roofs of
houses in the center of town; more than 200 survivors clam-
bered aboard seeking shelter. Warehouses, wharves, and taverns were swallowed up in a matter of seconds as huge fissures
appeared in the earth. More than 2,000 died in the cataclysm.
Although settlers had joined the town to the Palisadoes by
filling in the marshy swamps, Port Royal again became an
island. The 13 acres of land were rebuilt, only to be scorched
by fire in 1703, ending Port Royal's days of affluence. It did,
however, remain a thriving merchant community until it was
finally eclipsed by Kingston, and it remained as the Royal Navy's principal base in the Caribbean until the Navy abandoned it in 1905. Although the town was devastated by 1988's
Hurricane Gilbert, its main structures came through with flying colors.

sights: Dull gray, restored St. Peter's Church (1725) replaced
Christ Church, which sank into the sea during the 1692 earthquake. As you enter the building, a lady in her energetic eight-
ies will jump on you with a carefully rehearsed spiel and will
immediately point out Louis Galdy's plaque up on the wall.
Galdy, swallowed up during the 1692 cataclysm, was thrown
back up into the sea and survived. His tomb is in the churchyard. Other plaques commemorate sailors who died from yellow fever. Despite what you may be told, the silver communion
plate found here probably did not belong to Henry Morgan.
Nearby, Fort Charles, one of the oldest and best preserved of
the island's forts, now sits back a considerable distance from
the sea. Climb up on the quarterdeck to see where Horatio
Nelson paced back and forth in 1779 while waiting for a

French attack that never came. A small Maritime Museum has a surprisingly attractive collection of submarine cables, model ships, and information about 18th and 19th C. canoe making (open daily, 10–1, 2–5). Turn right at the Fort entrance and go straight to reach Giddy House, once the Royal Artillery Store. The National Museum of Historical Archaeology, at one time the Naval Hospital, has detailed archaeological exhibits, including Arawak artifacts, Samurai and Bedouin swords, a machete from Nanny Town, and bone wigcurlers excavated in Port Royal.

others: Port Royal is famous for its fried fish and bammy. Try Miss Gloria's Top and Bottom shops (two locations). Take a fishing boat out to Lime Cay (J$10 RT); boat will return for you in the afternoon. Beautiful snorkeling on this uninhabited island where Rhygin' the bandit, immortalized in the movie *The Harder They Come,* was gunned down by police. Negotiate to go out to other cays nearby. Gunboat Beach is along Palisadoes Rd. past the airport.

Spanish Town

Not only is Spanish Town the most historically fascinating of all Jamaica's towns, but its forthright, down-to-earth atmosphere makes it a pleasure to visit as well.

getting there: Take any bus marked "Spanish Town" from Half Way Tree for the half-hour, 20-km (12 mile) ride. From the bus station, go down Oxford St. and turn right and follow Wellington down to the Square. Spanish Town may also be approached from Port Henderson, Mandeville, Ocho Rios, or Linstead.

history: After the Spanish officially abandoned their first settlement at Sevilla la Nueva on the north coast in 1534, they established their capital here, calling it Villa de la Vega (town

Children on a swing, Port Royal

on the plain). Spanish Town was sacked several times by the English before being captured permanently in 1655. Enraged to find the town empty of valuables, conquering English troops burned and wrecked much of it. Later, Spanish town became the administrative hub of the island. Not only did the governor reside here, but the House of Assembly and the Courts of Justice were built here as well. A rivalry developed between Spanish Town and that upstart mercantile community, Kingston. Under the influence of unscrupulous Kingston merchants, the governor forced a bill through the legislature in 1755 which moved the capital to Kingston. Since the king had not assented to the bill, it was eventually proclaimed illegal. The reprieve was not permanent—and the capital was moved to Kingston permanently in 1872. As the plantation economy of the 19th C. withered away, so did the grandeur of Spanish Town.

sights: Cathedral Church of St. James, on Red Church St., stands on the site of the Spanish Chapel of the Red Cross which was destroyed by Cromwell's army. The rebuilt structure, converted to the Anglican sect, was destroyed by the 1712 hurricane. Reconstructed in 1714, the present weathered red brick structure is the second oldest (after Fort Charles) on the island. Step inside and see the inlaid marble tombs. Also check out the tombs in the peaceful courtyard outside, including those of George Washington Reed, an American who died as a POW in 1814; Sir Charles Price; and the inscribed tomb of Mrs. Mary Lewis, who died at age 18 in 1676. A public library is across the street. Only the facade remains of King's House, destroyed by fire in 1925 and now partially restored. Built in 1762, it was the center of the island's social life and history for more than 100 years until the capital was removed to Kingston. Abolition of slavery was proclaimed on 1 August 1838 from the steps of the portico. Walk in and see the out-door exhibits, including an old carriage and pimento fanner. Try to imagine that you're inside what was once considered to be the finest governor's residence in all of England's New World colonies. The Folk Museum has small but absorbing displays which link Jamaican culture with Amerindian (cassava), African (Yabbah bowls), and English (shingle-making) cultures.

SPANISH TOWN

1. Cathedral Church of St. James
2. King's House (Folk Museum)
3. House of Assembly
4. The Court House
5. Rodney Memorial/The National Archives
6. The Baptist Church
7. market
8. Post Office

The archaeological annex contains pottery shards and photos. The House of Assembly, across the street, was built in 1762 and has been frequently restored and altered. Street life goes on as usual in front of the pompous Rodney Memorial. The uncouth naval commander, cast in the role of Jamaica's savior because of his victory over the French in 1782, scowls sternly as he points with a scroll. Perhaps the fact that sculptor Bacon used Italian marble accounts for the fact that Rodney is wearing a Roman toga. (It is unclear as to whether or not they staged toga parties back in those days.) French cannon, the spoils of war, flank the statue. The remains of the Court House—which burned down in 1985—stand directly across the Square. The National Archives, located at the rear of the Rodney Memorial, has a small display including Moravian church documents, an old newspaper, and constitutional documents. The Baptist Church, corner William and French streets, built in 1827 and badly damaged during the 1951 hurricane, is associated with the famous missionary Phillippo. Its original congregation was composed of newly liberated slaves. The 18th C. barracks are nearby, and the first prefabricated cast iron bridge in the Americas (no longer in use) is along the road to Kingston. Streetside revival meetings with shaking tambourines and frenzied chanting take place outside the market. Inside, kerchief-clad ladies sell piles of chicken legs, bundles of kallaloo, and TDK T-shirts. A fish and bammy lady offers the genuine article behind the Rodney statue.

vicinity of Spanish Town: On the way to Kingston are the Cayamanas race track and the Arawak Indian Museum at White Marl. The latter has both indoor and outdoor displays of Indian remains and artifacts. To the north in the hills, Sligoville was once the summer home of the governor; it was established by the Baptist Rev. J. M. Phillippo. Purchasing the land in 1835, the town he started became the first post-emancipation free village in the W. Indies. Linstead is a celebrated market town. Guanaboa Vale, 15 km (nine miles) northwest of Spanish Town, has a church with interesting

Cathedral Church of St. James, Spanish Town

tombstones. A famous colonial mutiny occurred here in 1660.
Mountain River Cave, near the town, contains Arawak petro-
glyphs of hunters, birds, and turtles. Farther on to the north,
Lluidus Vale has a 300-year-old sugar plantation. At Old Harbour Bay west of Spanish Town, Columbus sighted manatees
for the first time, initially mistaking them for mermaids (Columbus was either extremely horny or extremely near-
sighted!). Little Goat I. offshore was a U.S. Naval Base from
1942–49. Colbeck Castle, 2.4 km northwest of Old Harbour, is
a mysterious building. Practically nothing is known of the origin of what was once the largest building on the island save
that it was built by the unpopular Col. John Colbeck in the
17th or 18th centuries. May Pen, an unappealing town of
40,000, is the capital of Clarendon Parish. To the south is Vere,
formerly (owing to its production of indigo dye) one of the most
prosperous districts in Jamaica. Once a separate parish, its
capital was Alley, whose church, St. Peter's (1715), is noted for
its bell and church organ. The entire courtyard is very English
in appearance. On the west bank of the Milk River to the
southwest of May Pen lies Milk River Bath, which has a radio-
activity level much higher than that of any other mineral spa
in the world. Reach here by taking transport from Four Paths
outside May Pen. Stay at the small hotel. Although they have
no phone, you can try reaching them through the Radio Room
at the Ministry of Public Works (tel. 923–6111) in Kingston.
Farquahr Beach is three km (almost two miles) to the south. A
track north of Milk River heads west along the coast to Alligator Pond. Porus, in the main road to Mandeville from May Pen,
is well-known for its citrus fruits.

Market, Spanish Town

THE BLUE
MOUNTAINS

Named for the haze that glazes their peaks the better part of each day, the Blue Mountains are undoubtedly the most unusual travel destination in Jamaica. Few people envision Jamaica as having cool woodlands, engulfed at times in a sea of heavy mist, but that is exactly what the Blue Mtns. have to offer. Forming the interior of Portland, St. Thomas, and St. Andrew, their consistently cool climate averages around 15° C (65°F). Heaved up from the floor of the Caribbean 25 million years ago, they are growing at a rate of one foot per thousand years. Dominating the Eastern Highlands, the Grand Ridge of the Blue Mountains contains many prominent peaks, all more than 1,640 m (5,000 ft.) and many are more than 1,968 m (6,000 ft.). From east to west, the peaks are Sugar Loaf, John Crow, and Silver Hill. Rounded, conical Blue Mountain Peak, highest on the island, is 2,256 m (7,402 feet). Once heavily timbered, the southern slopes of the Grand Ridge are being deforested at an alarming rate. The presence of rangers patrolling the terrain has not deterred local farmers who continue to clear land illegally in order to plant ganja and other crops. This is not the case with the side facing Portland, however, where torrential rainfall has left the rugged terrain virtually unexploited. Far to the east, the mountains collide with the much lower (3,000 ft.) John Crow Mountains. The Port Royal Mountains, a subsidiary range which affords Kingston its dramatic backdrop, run to the southeast.

getting there and around: A number of roads run around and through the mountains. A3, the main route to Annotto Bay, passes through Castleton, skirting the western edge. From Kingston a road runs up to the suburb of Jack's Hill and

on to Hollywell and other destinations. Another road on the
east side of Kingston heads up to The Cooperage, where it
splits to the east for Mavis Bank and Blue Mtn. Peak. The
west half of the fork leads on to Irish Town, Redlight, Newcastle, and Hardwar Gap before connecting with the road for Buff
Bay. These main routes are supplemented by innumerable
footpaths and shortcuts. Virtually no transport heads up this
way so unless you have your own vehicle, count on walking a
great deal.

practicalities: Places to stay and camp in this area are listed
in the text under specific localities. Cabins at Hollywell or
Clydesdale may be rented from the Forestry Department, 173
Constant Spring Rd., Kingston (tel. 42–667, 42–668). Reservations should be made one month in advance if planning to
arrive on a weekend. Although pots and pans are provided, it's
best to bring your own as they are occasionally stolen. For
Whitfield Hall Hostel reservations, phone John Algrove at
70986 or U.D.C. at 28310, 28314. Remember to bring your own
food, as restaurants and food stores, when available at all, are
few and far between.

Jack's Hill

No longer city but not yet country, this outlying suburb is a
great place to make the transition from urban to rural life. In
this small village, strung out along the side of the road, there's
little save a post office, bars and stores, a pay phone that is
perpetually out of order, an outdoor auto repair shop, and the
ubiquitous police station with the officers lazing about. There
are great views of Kingston, however, and magnificent sunsets
may be seen from the top of the water tower. Owing to the
irregular transportation, it's hardly a convenient place to stay
if interested in checking out Kingston's nightlife, through it's
a perfect place of departure for exploring the Blue Mountains.

To get here take a minivan or hitch up along steep Jack's Hill Rd. from the end of Kingston's Barbicon Road. A trail along Peter's Rock Rd. leads to Cambridge and then Hollywell and Hardwar Gap. Peter Bentley, head of SENSE Adventures, offers accommodations and day tours of the Blue Mtns. and Kingston. Peter Bentley's Maya Lodge is quiet and set in secluded natural environs. For "hostel" style accommodation, he charges US$10 pp.. Pillow, bottom sheet, and foam mattress are supplied. A room or cabin costs US$15 pn s and $25 d. Camping is US$7.50 pn with a $2.50 additional charge for each extra person. For more information call (809) 927-2097 or write Box 216, Kington 7. The only other accommodation up this way is the much pricier Ivor Guest House (tel. 927–1460).

Clydesdale and Cinchona

Clydesdale: Only an inoperative water wheel plus drying and roasting pits serve as a reminder that this seedling nursery was once a coffee plantation. A cabin rented out by the Forestry Dept. has the sayings of Rastafarian A. A. Peters featured on the walls inside. The kitchen and living room areas are attractively furnished. Bring all of your food and cooking supplies as none are available. Bathe in the river pool nearby. Trails lead to Morces and St. Helens Gaps.

Cinchona Botanic Gardens: Spectacularly set along a 1,527-m (5,000-ft.) ridge, Cinchona Botanic Gardens was named after the tree from whose bark quinine is obtained. Established as Cinchona and Assam tea plantation in 1868, it shrank over the years, as profits dwindled, to the small flower and vegetable garden which remains (although it is currently undergoing renovation). The numerous trees surrounding the great house are both indigenous and imported. Note the Blue Mtn. yacca with its small, dagger-shaped leaves. See workers picking coffee berries between Sept. and Feb. at the Silver Hill coffee factory (open daily 6–6).

getting there and vicinity: Take a No. 61 bus from Papine

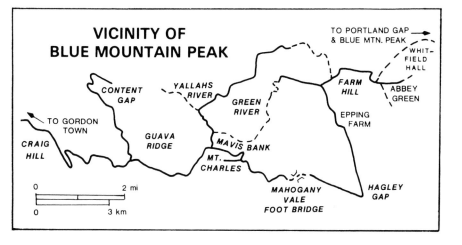

in Kingston up the steep, winding road to Guava Ridge via
The Cooperage. Nothing remains of Jamaica's first botanical
garden, established here in 1770. Follow the road along to
Content Gap and try some free samples on the way at "World's
End," a distillery run by Scottish immigrant Ian Sangster.
From Content Gap the left path from the water tower leads to
Charlottenburg House, an old great house. Keep straight from
Content Gap to St. Peters and Clydesdale.

Blue Mountain Peak

One of the highlights of any trip in the Blue Mtns. is climbing
up Blue Mountain Peak. It's best to overnight at Whitfield
Hall before attempting the strenuous three-hour climb. Most
hikers rise in the dead of night (2–3 AM) to begin the ascent in
order to arrive at the top in time to view the resplendent sunrise. On a clear morning it's possible to see as far as Cuba. The
forest along the way is composed of short, gnarled colorado
trees, their branches laden with mosses, epiphytes, and ferns.
At their bases look for enchanting dwarf orchids. The upper
wet montane and elfin forests here are classic.

practicalities   Take a minibus from Papine to Mavis Bank. Then follow the 10-km bridle path from Mavis Bank to Whitfield Hall. Whitfield Hall Hostel, near the village of Penlye Castle, has dorm beds (including a crib). It's cheaper if you stay in your own tent. Have a look over the marvelous collection of antique books on the shelves of this simply but attractively furnished home, which was once the great house of a coffee plantation. Meals are served here upon request. Bring all food, a flashlight, sweater, and rain parka.

Newcastle and Hollywell

Newcastle: Take the main road from Kingston past Irish Town to get to this Jamaica Defence Force Camp set high in the hills overlooking the Mamee River Valley. Established in 1814 as a hill station for British troops at a time when, owing to the prevalance of disease, a sojourn on the coast was regarded as a certain death sentence, this former coffee plantation was gradually built up into the present day red-roofed buildings. The bar and Sergeant's Mess are available for use by visitors.

Hollywell: Situated 2^1/$_2$ miles from Newcastle at 990 m (3,250 ft.) and covering an extensive 300 acres (120 ha), this forest reserve includes picnic tables and miles of hiking trails. An excellent place to stay for a few days and take day hikes, three cabins are for rent here. Cabin No. 1 has two bedrooms; the other three cabins are equipped with twin beds. Campers must *also* be renting a cabin. All reservations must be made and prepaid at the Forestry Department in Kingston.

Castleton: The main road from Kingston to Annotto Bay passes through these gardens. Established in 1859, time and the continual flooding of the Wag Water River have reduced its

Mango peddler, Blue Mountains

splendor. One the richest botanical garden in the entire Caribbean, it's still well worth a visit. Strychnos trees, from which strychnine is obtained, stand in the upper section of the garden. Mahogany and Burmese teak may be seen in the lower section (open 7–6 daily).

SOUTH AND WEST JAMAICA

MANDEVILLE

A fairly large, extremely scattered town, this is the capital of Manchester Parish. Although Mandeville has long been compared to an English country town, its Continental character is swiftly fading as it becomes a carbon copy of American suburbia with shopping centers and Kentucky Fried Chicken. The area surrounding the Manchester Club, which has the island's oldest golf course, still retains a distinctly English feeling. Although at the time of its establishment in 1814 it was a playground for landed European gentry, expatriates today are predominantly Americans working in the bauxite industry, which has brought relative prosperity to this area. Mandeville is definitely a place to beat the heat; the temperature here ranges from the 60s during the winter to the 70s during the summer. To really experience the town in all its radiance, get out in the early morning and take in the special qualities of the sunlight. The area's most famous product is the *ortanique*. Developed here about 1920 by C. P. Jackson, the name for this seedless, extremely juicy fruit was coined by combining the words "orange, tangerine and unique."

getting there and around: Most easily reached by bus or minibus from Kingston (via Spanish Town) or from Black River. Or take a train to Williamsfield from Montego Bay or Kingston, then a minibus or shared taxi on to Mandeville.

There's no local bus system so you'll either have to walk or bargain with the drivers of shared taxis.

Sights

downtown: All of the major streets slope up to Mandeville Square where the park, market, courthouse and rectory are located. Surrounded by a sea of modernity, the anachronistic courthouse was built with limestone blocks cut by slaves. Completed around 1820, the design underwent many modifications before it was finished. Standing to the left of the courthouse, what was once Mandeville's rectory is still the oldest house in town. Rented out as a tavern, it was later used as a guest house before being converted to a private residence. Also on the central green, Manchester Parish Church opened its doors in 1820. Mandeville Hotel, an old landmark on Hotel St., was originally a barracks for English troops before being converted to a hotel during the 1890s. It has long been a place of retirement for many expatriate British.

Paul Cross Nursery: Run by Charles Dougherty, a down-to-earth Catholic priest from New Jersey, this nursery is a self-help project and cultivates 2^1/$_2$ acres of plants for export to the US. Preeminent among these is the anthurium, a tropical flower which has recently gained in popularity in the US and Europe. Grown in coconut husks, these Hawaiian natives can last five days without water after harvest and up to a month in a flower vase. While they fetch the nursery only 90 Jamaican cents each, they can sell for up to US$36 a dozen Stateside. The courtyard-enclosed garden features a variety of orchids and a garden with lily pond. There's also a nursery school and health clinic in operation here. Interdenominational retreats are held on the grounds as well. A J$10 donation is requested. It's located on Manchester Rd. near Newleigh Rd.

Mrs. Stephenson's Garden: This sweet lady has been cultivating her garden for 12 years now. Carmen grows anthuriums, ortanique, citrus, and orchids, and her horticultural products generally take the bulk of the awards at the annual horticultural fair. A J$10 donation is request. The garden is off New Green Rd. on the way to Winston Jones Highway.

bammy factory: This is run out of Clem Bloomfield's home. The manufacture of these cassava cakes was learned from the Indians. It's an intricate process of grinding, pressing, roasting, and scraping. The cakes, of course, form half the ingredients of the traditional dish "fish and bammy." He's located off Greenvale Rd. between West Rd. and Winston Jones Highway. Check with the tourist office or the Astra for current tour availability.

Marshall's Pen: This 18th C. great house is set inside a 300-acre cattle farm. Purchased by Arthur Sutton in 1939, it is also a preserve for birds. While the affable Suttons offer tours of their house and opportunities for birdwatching on the grounds, their main business is rearing cattle. They care for Red Poll calves until they are 10 months old and then sell them; their calves are so popular that there is a three-year waiting period. The Suttons live in the main house—once the center of a coffee plantation—and have endeavored to furnish it appropriately. The charge for tours is J$30 pp. (tel. 962–2260). Birdwatching tours of the estate (98 species reported seen) and to the Cockpit Country are also available but must be arranged in advance.

Cecil Charlton's Mansion: Manchester Green Farm and Stables, located 2.5 km south of town atop Huntingdon Summit, appears from the distance to be a gigantic futuristic green Chinese pagoda—almost as if a spacecraft full of Oriental aliens had landed on top of the hill. Horses and cows graze on the green, fenced-in pastures along the way up to this octagonal mansion owned by Mandeville's mayor and former sno-cone salesman Cecil Charleton. Outside, birdcages containing cockatoos and other tropical exotics hang near a fountain built in the shape of a map of Jamaica and a walkway representing the Jamaican flag. An outdoor swimming pool flows under the walls into the living room where it transforms into a small pond. Get permission to view the estate; tel. 962–2247/2493.

others: Two other places to visit are the small High Mountain Coffee Factory (tel. 962–4211) and the Pioneer Chocolate Factory (tel. 962–4216/4276). The coffee factory is located up the street from the Williamsfield train depot. As they only roast the beans, there isn't much to see. To find the chocolate plant, cross the tracks and head down the road; the train station and a small craft store should be on your left. Turn right past the gas station and follow the wafting, exotically bitter odor of roasting chocolate down a winding road with a fence to find the factory. During the free and very informative tour, you'll be shown the various processes involved, ending with the chocolate bars, still inside molds, rattling down the production line.

Practicalities

accommodations: Mandeville Hotel (tel. 962–2138), at 4 Hotel St., is a local institution run in style by the affable McIntyre clan. Currently at the helm, manager Gordon McIntyre has been striving diligently to upgrade facilities and service. There are 60 double rooms and some self-contained units available. Set off from the road, it's in its own special, peaceful world—one which is just a matter of minutes from the center of action. In addition to a pool, there's a fine restaurant and bar. Gordon particularly welcomes "golden agers." Complimentary features include transportation to and from Williamsfield Station, early morning coffee or tea, and a free welcome drink at the bar. Located outside of the town's core, The Astra, managed by Diana McIntyre-Pike, Gordon's vivacious and dynamic sister, has a functional simplicity which gives it a personal grace. Originally a 10-room apartment building, it was converted by Mr. and Mrs. Conway McIntyre into a hotel catering to expatriates at work in the bauxite industry. There are two bars: one inside and one poolside. Imbibe your complimentary "welcome drink" at either. A "Revival Room" next to the pool is perfect for meetings. Diana McIntyre has a special concept, one unfortunately all too rare in the impersonal, unimaginative world of Jamaican tourism, Her "Community Tourism" involves bringing the local citizens into contact with visitors. This affords visitors the opportunity to experience life as the locals live it and the chance for Jamaicans to meet North Americans and Europeans at first hand and not only via the boob tube. She hopes to prevent the type of unplanned development that has marred both Negril and the North Coast. In conjunction with this effort, Diana and brother Gordon invite locals and high school students into their hotels so that they can understand what the hotel business and tourism is all about. In order to make her visitors feel right at home in the community, she takes them around and about for a complimentary tour. Ask Diana about her up-and-coming bed and breakfast program. Visitors will pay around US$30 for a single or double room. She can also arrange a rental car which will be immediately available upon arrival.

budget accommodations: Try the Rodan Guest House (tel. 962–2552), Wesley Rd.. The International Chinese Hotel (tel. 962–0527) is at 17 Manchester Rd.. Outside Mandeville in Christiana, the Villa Bella (tel. 964–2243) offers 18 rooms for J$150 s and J$225 d. Rates include breakfast.

dining out: Worth a visit even if you aren't in the mood for something to eat or drink, Bill Lauries's Mandeville Steak House is a local institution. Commanding a panoramic view of Mandeville from its hilltop location, its interior is filled with memorabilia assembled by collector extraordinaire Laurie. In existence at this location since 1972, the restaurant and its porch house everything from an international collection of 500-plus license plates (from the Dutch Caribbean to "Washington D.C. 1981 Presidential Inauguration") to a collection of cast iron items or a hanging Goodyear blimp. Other memorabilia include a hundred-year-old telephone, a 1923 Panatron gramophone, and a functional Caledonia wood burning stove in the kitchen. There's also a collection of antique cars. This steakhouse was known as the Bloomfield Hotel until the

MANDEVILLE AND SOUTH COAST ACCOMMODATIONS

KEY: S = Single; D = Double; 3rd = Third person sharing; S1 = 10% service charge; BA = Private bath/shower; P = Pool; B = Beach on property or in vicinity; EP = European Plan (no meals); CP = Continental Plan (breakfast included); MAP = Modified American Plan (breakfast and dinner included)

NOTE: Rates (in US$) are given as a guideline only; price fluctuations can and will occur. Summer season generally runs 4/15–11/15 or 12/15; check with hotel concerned for specifics. Hotel tax is levied on each room regardless of the number of people staying in it.

ADDRESS/ TELEPHONE	WINTER			SUMMER			# OF ROOMS	NOTES
	S	D	ROOM TAX	S	D	ROOM TAX		
The Astra Hotel, Box 60, Mandeville (62 Ward Avenue), 962-3265/3377	45–90		8	45–90		4	18	BA, P, EP
Hotel Pontio, Box 35, Mandeville (High St.), 965-2255	Inquire		4	24–39	56	2	12	S1, BA, B, EP
Mandeville Hotel, Box 78, Mandeville (4 Hotel St.), 962–2460/2138	40–90		4	40–90		2	60	S1, BA, P, EP
Natania's Guest House, Little Culloden, White House P.O., Westmoreland	40			40			8	BA, B, EP
South Sea View Guest House, White House P.O., Westmoreland	Inquire			40				
Treasure Beach Hotel, Box 5, Black River, St. Elizabeth, 965-2305	Inquire			40	50	16		BA, P, B, EP
Villa Bella Hotel, Christiana PO, Manchester, 964-2243				40	60	16		BA, CP
Wilton Guest House, Bluefields, Westmoreland	70	120		70	120		4	BA, MAP

1950s. Cuisine ranges in price from Pumpkin Soup (J$6.50) up to a US tenderloin steak (J$68.80). The best hotel dining is to be found at the Mandeville Hotel and the Astra. Both of these are renowned for service and hospitality.

budget dining: A good value for the atmosphere is the Pot-pourri Restaurant across the street from the Odeon Cinema. Its dishes run the gamut from hotdogs to bacon & eggs, from curried goat to sweet and sour pork. Also try the Miami Vice club and the Capri nearby. Miss Bennett's Fish Hut at Caledonia Plaza has breakfast from J$8 and charges J$15–20 for fish dishes. For Chinese food, the International Chinese Restaurant is reasonable. Housed in two 20-year-old converted buses on Perthwood St., Buss Stop serves local cuisine; there's no other place like it on the island. For baked goods try the Sunshine Bakery housed next to the Yokohama Betting Shop on Manchester Rd.. Ice cream is served at Krispy Kones near the Odeon. For baked goods, Lynn's Bakery is on Ward Avenue. Marzouca's Deli, in Mandeville Plaza, has pickled, sinful-tasting Satan's Sauce and Pepperwind Pepper Jelly, used for seasoning meat. Also available are *dulce* (guava cheese) and guava liqueur. For grocery shopping try Bravo Enterprises at 7B Caledonia Rd., Phildon Serve All at 5 Manchester Rd., Landem Discount at 41 Manchester Rd., Mandeville Cash 'N' Carry at Midway Plaza, and Urvill's Shop 'N' Save at 32 Manchester Rd.. The Basic Mini Mart stands next to the Odeon Theatre.

entertainment: The most fun thing to do during the daytime is to watch the man playing a musical saw on Main St. across from the "Get Signs and Tombstones Made to Order Here" sign. Planet Video Disco (tel. 962–0360), 10 Mandeville Plaza, features large screen video movies nightly except Sun. at 8. Mon. they show the "weekend preview", Tues. a "blue movie", Wed. and Thurs. a comedy; and the Mon. film is repeated on Fri. and Saturdays. After the movie, they play disco, soul, reggae, and calypso. If you bring a group, they will cater to your needs. Admission ranges from J$3–10. Other discos in the same area include Coney Island and Tracks. Zeex is out at Caledonia Plaza.

shopping: Located behind Manchester Plaza, the SWA Craft Centre (tel. 962–2138) offers employment to young unemployed women who lack skills. After they are trained, they can go on to work for themselves. Here, embroidery work, crochet, toys, clothing, and baked goods are for sale. These not only make good souvenirs, they put money where it's needed. Check out their line of cute Rastafarian dolls. Mandeville's extremely colorful market is set off to one side of Mandeville Square, housed in a yellow building. Squatting higglers flow out the doors onto the sloping driveway along the entrance where they sell yams, green peppers, cassava, white turnips, oranges, green bananas, ginger, beans and sugarcane. Also outside there's usually a revivalist group present with a lady, wearing a white turban, reading from the Bible and holding a white flag. Inside, the meat market has individually apportioned stalls with cow and goat heads for sale. Fishes of all sizes, shapes and colors are sold from tin washing pans.

services and information: The Tourist Board office (tel 962–1072) is at 21 Ward Ave., open 8:30–4:30, Mon. to Fri.. The local branch of Jamaica Information Service is across from NCB on Caledonia Plaza. Another excellent source for information is Diana McIntyre-Pike at the Hotel Astra, tel 962–3265/3377. Drugstores include Bennett's at 25 Main St.; Bravo Enterprises, 7B Caledonia Rd.; Hargreaves, 32 Hargreaves Ave.; Haughton's, 18 West Park Crescent; Grove Court in Grove Court Shopping Centre; and Fontana in Manchester Plaza Shopping Centre. Bookland is at Manchester Shopping Centre. In case you would like to be helped by the relative of a leading luminary, you can visit Seaga's sister at her Global Travel in Manchester Shopping Centre.

sports: Over 120 years old, the Manchester Club is the oldest private club in the Caribbean. Its facilities include billiards, tennis and golf; the 9 hole course is Jamaica's oldest. Facilities are available to guests of the Astra and Mandeville hotels. John S. Nightingale (tel. 962–2822,) 13 Perth Rd, offer horseback rides—a perfect thing to do in Mandeville!

from Mandeville: Buses and minibuses leave regularly for Black River and Montego Bay. For Treasure Beach take a minibus as far as Santa Cruz and then change. If taking the train to Montego Bay or Kingston, call up the train station in Williamsfield (tel. 962–4213).

Vicinity of Mandeville

The whole area surrounding Mandeville has much to offer. Since it's unfrequented by tourists or visitors, you're pretty far off the beaten track, so finding transport may be difficult. This is one area where it would be worthwhile to rent a car.

to the north: The bauxite mining operation of Alcan's Kirkvine Works dominates the valley to the northeast of Mandeville. Tours can be arranged by phone. From the top of Shooter's Hill near the plant, a splendid panorama unfolds with Blue Mountain Peak clearly visible to the east. The Pickapeppa factory, home of Jamaica's famous version of Worcestershire Sauce, is at the crossroads of Rtes. B4, 5, and 6. Mile Gully has an attractive 19th C. church, while Grove Place has the largest livestock breeding research station on the island. Situated at 846-m (2,750-ft.) elevation about three km north of Christiana is Gourie Recreation Center (enter near Coleyville Banana Plant). With an average mean temperature of 68° F, Gourie is an attractive place to stay for relief from the heat. In addition to numerous hiking trails, there's also the Gourie Cave, source of the Black River.

to the south: Marlborough House, at Spur Tree, built in 1795, is a fine example of a late 18th C. Palladian great house. Ask permission to visit. Get a fantastic view from the Alcan parking lot at the top of Spur Tree Hill. Alligator Pond, a quiet fishing village, has an early morning fish market. Locals rent out cottages. Unless you're driving a jeep, plan to walk the 30 km (18 miles) through aptly named Gut River to Milk River. Off to one side of the road is God's Well, a 50-m (160-ft.)-deep limestone sinkhole with sparkling turquoise water. It was named by a man who claimed to have been cured of a terminal illness by bathing here. You might see manatees at Cano Valley.

THE SOUTHWEST COAST

Treasure Beach

This gem of a beach area is located in one of Jamaica's remotest regions. Almost completely isolated with no phones or newspapers and little rainfall, four small bays (Great, Calabash, Frenchman's, and Billy's) are connected by road with the small town of Treasure Beach. Yellow and red fishing boats line the brown sand beach at Calabash Bay. Frenchman's Bay has the best beach, though it's crowded Sundays. Good hiking in this area—especially along the bluff from Great Bay. Locals, some of whom are said to be the descendants of shipwrecked Scottish seamen, are among the friendliest in all Jamaica. Most famous of them is Chrissie James, a basketmaker who won the Jamaica 21 competition, held in celebration of the island's independence.

getting there: From Mandeville take a minibus to Santa Cruz, then change to a vehicle for Pedro Cross or Treasure Beach. Or approach from Mountainside or the smaller of the two Lacovias. Transportation is extremely irregular, so count on long waits both ways.

practicalities: A great variety of houses are for rent here. Prices are lowest on weekdays. Try the Four M's Cottage run

by Mrs. Effie Campbell. Treasure Beach Resort Hotel takes tourists from the states, misinforming them that the beach is private and suitable for nudism. It isn't! Locals are greatly offended by nudism so watch it. Great Bay Coop is the best-stocked shop in the area. Weekly markets are held in Cala-bash and Great Bays on Fridays. Buy fresh fish and lobster directly from fishermen; the best time is from 12 to 1 Mon. and Friday.

Black River

The curving A2 highway runs right through this pretty town set along the coast, dividing the sea from the deteriorating but colorful gingerbread houses. This sleepy fishing village, once a major logging center, explodes with color and activity on Fri. and Sat. when the covered market is held. Crocodiles still lurk upriver. For salt water swimming, continue on to Belmont and Bluefields beaches. Try the peppered shrimp at Middlequar-ters, 13 km (eight miles) south. The Holland Estate and sugar factory is near the junction of A2 and the oddly named Y.S. River with its Y.S. Falls. Find the overrated "Bamboo Ave-nue," a stretch of bamboo-shaded road acclaimed as a tourist attraction on the way to Lacovia. Stop for refreshments at the Traveler's Halt. To view rum production, visitors may tour the Appleton Estate.

practicalities: Natania's Guest House at Little Culloden is the most renowned accommodation. The Hotel Pontio is on Main St. in Black River. (See chart for rates). The South Sea View Guest House can be booked through Ms. Rubin at (212) 633–8996. For other accommodation, try the Port of Call Hotel (tel. 965–2360/2410), 136 Crane Rd., and the Bridge House Hotel (tel. 965–2361), 14 Crane Rd.. For food, try the restau-rants in the Port of Call and in the Bridge House Hotel.

river tours: Personable Charles Swaby (tel. 962–0220/3351, 965–2206/2513) is the Managing Director of South Coast Safa-

ris Ltd. which conducts boat tours of the Black River. He has great enthusiasm for the local crocodiles—so much so that he houses several of them in concrete pens in back of his house on Hotel St. in Mandeville.

Savanna-La-Mar

The name of this undistinguished sugar port means "plain by the sea." Few towns in the world have been devastated more frequently by hurricanes than Sav-La-Mar. The 1748 hurricane left ships beached, the 1780 hurricane completely destroyed the town, and the one in 1912 cast the schooner *Laconia* into the middle of the main street. Not much to see here except the fort which has long served as an improvised swimming pool. In 1755 a visiting admiral declared it to be the very worst fort on the island. From Bluefields to the south, Henry Morgan sailed to sack Panama in 1670. A small sand beach skirts the white bay here. At Pelican Hole, near the bridge over the Bluefields River, two enormous birches and a fig tree shelter pelicans, frigate birds and boobies. Some crumbling walls still stand at Oristan where Spaniards founded the short-lived settlement of Oristan in 1509. Rumored to have been built to house Napoleon, the ruined 19th-C. castle on the grounds of Auchindown Farm was built by one Archibald Campbell. Its two towers are—rather absurdly—connected underground. See the early morning fish market at Whitehouse where dugout canoes are still constructed.

accommodations: Wilton Guest House is at Bluefields. (See chart for rates). San Michele and Mullion Cove are two fully staffed luxury beach houses with tennis courts and pools which are rented out on a weekly basis. For information write C. Braxton Moncure, 116 North Saint Asaph St., Alexandria, VA 22314, tel. (703) 549–5276. Located near Petersfield to the

Treasure Beach

northeast, The Blue Hole View, a restaurant and spice farm at the source of the Roaring River, offers simple rooms and campsites.

THE WESTERN INTERIOR

Seaford Town

Near the village of Rat Trap stands what is probably Jamaica's most unusual village—the only one consisting almost entirely of fair-skinned blue-eyed farmers. First settled by a band of 570 from Bremen, Germany, in 1835, another thousand or so came to settle during the succeeding eight years. Created a baron in 1826, Lord Seaford granted 500 acres of his Westmoreland estate in response to a government plea for more land grants to encourage European immigration to replace slave labor. Although each immigrant was granted from three to 23 acres, the land was mountainous and lacked irrigation water—basically unarable. Free rations were provided by the Jamaican government for the first 18 months, but the settlers had to walk 19 km to Chester Castle to pick them up. Population plummeted under the effects of malnutrition and yellow fever, but the hardy Germans stayed on. In recent years the population has decreased because of emigration. Inbreeding has reduced the number of family names to only 15 with Kameke being the most prominent. Although there has been interbreeding with blacks, most of these marriages were with younger sons and daughters of the community who, lacking the right to inherit land, chose to settle outside. Although a few houses of distinctive architectural style and some customs remain, no living soul here can speak a word of German. A museum near the Sacred Heart Catholic Church contains a list of family names and other memorabilia.

Cockpit Country

formation: Viewed from the air, this potholed limestone plateau resembles nothing so much as a series of meshed cardboard egg containers covered with a green carpet of vegetation. Stretching over a 500-sq-mile area, it covers the southern half of Trelawny Parish and extends over to the east edge of St. James and then down to the northern tip of St. Elizabeth. The enormous, craggy limestone pits that give the region its name are a result of a unique geological process called karstification. Just five million years ago the terrain was flat. Over a million-year period, heavy rains seeped through the primary structural lines and joints of the porous limestone terrain, carving huge caves, deep sinkholes, and long underground passages. Now lush, verdant vegetation masks the treacherous pits. Inaccessible to all but the hardiest adventurer, they remain virtually unexplored even today.

the Maroons: The only group of people to ever attempt to tame the pits did so out of sheer necessity. These people were the Maroons. After the British invaded Jamaica in 1655, it took five years to crush the last armed Spanish resistance. During this period, African slaves, left to their own resources, took to the inaccessible areas of the Cockpit country and the Blue Mountains, grouping together for self-defense. Around 1662 they became known as the Maroons. No one is certain of the name's derivation, but it's thought to have come from the French *marron,* which means "runaway slave." Another possibility is that it might be a corruption of the Spanish *cimarran,* meaning "wild or untamed." The Maroons were able to exist in the harsh environment of the cockpits because some of the pit bottoms were flat and tillable. Many are as large as baseball fields; the site of Petty River Bottom, a former Maroon camp, measures seven acres. Maroon settlements in the Blue Mountains and in the cockpits became havens for runaway slaves. Soon, a guerrilla war began which stretched over 80 years. In 1663 the British attempted to settle with the implacable Maroons, but an envoy sent to sue for peace was cut to pieces instead. From 1690 to 1720, Maroons raided plantations for livestock and goods. The British responded by organizing bands of armed slaves and importing Indians from Cuba to go after the Maroons. The Maroons were split into two groups: the Leeward Maroons led by Kojo (or Kudjoe), and the Windward Maroons in Portland Parish, led by Quao, Kofi, and the legendary Nanny (see "Nannytown" under "Vicinity of Port Antonio").

Maroon autonomy: Conceding defeat at last in 1738, the British signed a peace treaty with Kojo on 1 March 1739. Legal autonomy (which theoretically stands to this day) was granted along with ownership of 2,500 acres to be used for farming and hunting. The Windward Maroons signed an agreement shortly thereafter. The role of the Maroons changed dramatically from that of protectors of runaway slaves to slave hunters. Called in to suppress rebellions, Maroons killed the rebel leader Tacky Blue in 1760. But the peace did not last forever. In 1759, in clear violation of a treaty provision stating that only Maroons could administer justice to Maroons, two Trelawny Maroons were whipped after being caught red-handed stealing a pig in Montego Bay. This incident, coupled with a desire for more land, incited the community to war again. The 600 Trelawnys were met by a force of 1,500 British troops equipped with Cuban bloodhounds; these terrifying dogs caused the Maroons to sue for peace. Agreeing to the Maroon's stipulation that they were not to be executed or transported, they were instructed by the government to surrender within a few days. After the last of them had straggled in on 21 March, the governor declared that treaty conditions had been violated and shipped them off to Halifax, Nova Scotia. After four harsh winters, they were sent to Sierra Leone on the W. coast of Africa. Although Trelawny Town has disappeared, the old Maroon Town Barracks remain at Flagstaff near Maroon Town. Fascinating to visit. Nowadays, there's little to differentiate the Maroon from any other Jamaican. Rasta influence and television have taken their toll, and a police station now stands in the chief Leeward Maroon settlement of Accompong.

Accompong: A beaten and pitted road leads up to this primitive mountain village, named after Maroon leader Kojo's brother. Most of the people here are descendants of the Akan-speaking peoples of W. Africa. A schoolteacher and preacher, Col. Harris Cawley is the leader of these Maroons, who celebrate Kojo's birthday here every 6 January. Complex drumming commences at daybreak, and the villagers make a pilgrimage to Accompong's grave and the *ceiba* tree where the treaty with the British was signed. The day's celebration ends with a reggae dance party in the evening. Currently, Col. Harris Cawley is demanding a confederation. He wants the Jamaican government to fly the Maroon flag alongside the Jamaican one and has called on the UN for recognition. He claims that the British disregarded Maroon sovereignty when drafting the constitution and objects to Nanny's being made a national heroine without consulting the Maroons.

THE WEST COAST

Negril

On the southwest tip of Westmoreland Parish and protected by an offshore reef, this 11-km stretch of sand is one of the finest beaches in the Caribbean. Wade out to your waist in crystal-clear water the color of emeralds; see right down to the white sand bottom. Once a traveler's paradise, Negril now qualifies as an up-and-coming Miami Beach, well on the way to holding the dubious distinction of being the worst tourist trap on the island. It has become a ghetto for middle- and upper-class North Americans and Europeans, imitation Rastas, and home to at least half of the hawkers of tourist services (the other half base themselves at MoBay and Ocho Rios). Just walk along the beach for a moment and they're on you like flies:

"Anything to drink? Banana Bread? Tie your hair into braids? Want to see a real Jamaican pussy, man?" Sundays are the worst because the kids are all out of school. Avoid hassles by walking in or along the water, wearing earplugs, or turning your Walkman up full blast. Another option might be to lie on the beach and lay out one beer, a piece of banana bread, some fruit, and a ganja spliff. Then you *might* be left alone. Another alternative is to come during the dry season, when higglers disappear like mosquitoes. Remember, however, this is how they make their daily *ackee*, and if you don't mind being in the center of an 11-km outdoor market, Negril is a great place!

history: Originally named Negrillo by the Spanish. In 1702 Admiral Benbow assembled his squadron for a voyage which ended with his defeat by the French. Captain Barnet captured pirate Calico Jack—so named because of his passion for calico underwear—along with his female crew members here in 1702. In 1814, the British flotilla left from here for New Orleans.

Negril

Negril was redeveloped at a cost of US$4.5 million in 1973 when a new highway and drainage canals were constructed. Around the same time, arriving hippies founded the site of Ganjaland on a forested track near the airport. Turning capitalist in the latter half of the '70s, they were responsible for bringing development to Negril.

getting there: Easily approached by minibus or bus from MoBay, Lucea, or Sav-La-Mar. In fact, owing to the persistence of touts who pack the minibuses, you may end up going there whether you intend to or not. **by air:** Trans Jamaican flies here from Montego Bay.

accommodations: Most of these were damaged (if not devastated) by 1988's Hurricane Gilbert but the majority have been rebuilt or repaired. The more famous hotels include Negril Gardens, Negril Beach Club, Poinciana Beach Hotel, Sundowner, and T—Water Beach Hotel. (See chart for rates). Rockhouse (tel. 957-4373) is a cluster of thatched roof cottages. Each is equipped with hot plate and refrigerator. For reservations write Box 78, Park Ridge, IL 60068. The Negril Palm Beach Club (tel. 957-4218) has 12 rooms with private bath. Home Sweet Home (Box 2, Negril, Jamaica tel. 957-4478) has private rooms and cottages on the sea. For information, phone (419) 947-1193. Also try The Bungalo (tel. 957-4400) on Norman Manley Blvd. Bar-B-Barn (tel. 957-4267) is on the beach. Rock Cliff Club (tel. 957-4331) has bedrooms and suites with a/c and private balconies overlooking the Caribbean. For info Stateside phone 1-800-423-4095 or 1-800-243-9420. Seatop Resort (tel. 957-4308, 955-2840) is on Lighthouse Rd. For information call (718) 287-3618.

villas: For a range of lodgings, contact Hilltop Villas and Apartments, (tel. 957-4253), Hermitage Road. Our Past Time Villas (tel. 974-4224), is located on Norman Manley Blvd. at Rutland Point. Sandi San Beach Villas (tel. 957-4487), Norman Manley Blvd. Also try Coral Cove Villas (tel. 957-4454), Lighthouse Rd. Negrillo Cottages (tel. 957-4493) offers two-bedroom villas. Another is White Sands Villas (tel. 957-4291). Palm Grove Resort (tel. 957-4461/4427), on the cliffs at West End, offers two- and three-bedroom villas. Dream Scape Villa (tel. 957-4495) features satellite TV, refrigerators, room service, and complimentary breakfasts. Emerald Lodge (tel. 957-4426) has 16 cottages. Milestone Cottages (tel. 957-4442), West End Rd., features one- and two-bedroom cottages. Dollhouse Cottages (Box 6, tel. 957-4282) is on the beach. Falcon Cottages (Box 20, tel. 957-4263) has villas available. Rondel Village (tel. 957-4413) has octogonal shaped villas with whirlpools, satellite TV, and maid service. Yellow Bird Sea-Tel (tel. 957-4252) has five two-bedroom cottages with fans, kitchen, living-dining area, and a patio. Write Irene Hansen, Centralia, MO 65240 or call (314) 682-2505. Native Son Villas (tel. 957-4376) consists of fully-staffed villas on the beach with one and two bedrooms (one has three bedrooms). For reservations Stateside call (201) 467-1407. Summerset Village (tel. 957-4346), consisting of a number of cottages and bungalows two miles from the beach, provides fan, kitchen facilities, maid service, and a pool. For reservations phone 1-800-423-4095 or (312) 883-1020. Crystal Water Villas (tel. 957-4284), situated

Negril Rock House

along the middle of the beach, has one- to three-bedroom villas with kitchen, a/c, maid service, and security. Call 212-759-1025 or 1-800-433-3020 Stateside for reservations. Negril Yoga Centre (tel. 957-4397) has rustic cottages with fans, maid service, refrigerators, and vegetarian meals upon request.

budget accommodations: Run by Ray and Elaine Arthurs, Arthurs Golden Sunset (tel. 957-4241) is famous for hospitality and fine authentic meals. Their detached buildings have shared kitchen and bath. During peak season, they host concerts and parties under the stars. They charge $30–50 per night per room with a 33 percent discount during the off season. Contact them at Box 21, Negril. The best way to find an inexpensive room is to state your price range and ask around; it should be easier to find a bargain during peak season. Other accommodation includes Bill's Paradise (PO Box 3, tel. 957-4346); Gold Nugget, (tel. 957-4388), Norman Manley Blvd; Lighthouse Park (Box 3, tel. 957-4346) which has camping, cottages, and bamboo cabanas; and Silver Sand Restaurant & Bar (tel. 957-4207) which has rooms for rent. Firefly also has inexpensive accommodation and camping. For other places to pitch a tent, try inquiring along the beach. Spring Garden Bed & Breakfast (tel. 957-4323) is located halfway to Sav-la-Mar near New Hope.

dining out and food: The cuisine here is good at most hotels but expensive when compared to *Ital* places in the market such as Ital Vital, One Stop, and Livity. But be aware that the latter close early. Arthurs is worth the prices for its food and atmosphere. Fisherman's Cafe, across the road nearby, has very reasonable prices. Among the most famous West End eateries along Lighthouse Road are Rick's Cafe and Charela Inn. The latter features French and Jamaican cuisine and has an extensive wine list. Chicken Lavish has the best chicken and other food at reasonable prices. Also try the Silver Star Cafe—which features an all-day breakfast, sandwiches, and Italian cuisine—or Sundowner's which has a buffet. Archway Cafe serves pizza, chicken & chips, fish & chips, spaghetti, and other American cuisine. Rock Cliff Club has all you can eat dinners on Thurs. and Sun. nights. Mariners Inn is also at the

NEGRIL ACCOMMODATIONS

KEY: S = Single; D = Double; 3rd = Third person sharing; S1 = 10% service charge; BA = Private bath/shower; P = Pool; B = Beach on property or in vicinity; EP = European Plan (no meals); CP = Continental Plan (breakfast included); AI = All inclusive
NOTE: Rates (in US$) are given as a guideline only; price fluctuations can and will occur. Summer season generally runs 4/15–11/15 or 12/15; check with hotel concerned for specifics. Hotel tax is levied on each room regardless of the number of people staying in it.

ADDRESS/ TELEPHONE	WINTER			SUMMER			# OF ROOMS	NOTES
	S	D	ROOM TAX	S	D	ROOM TAX		
Addis Kokeb, West End Road, Negril, 957-4485	35–65	40–70		25–50	30–50		5	S1, BA, B
Charela Inn, Box 33, Negril, 957-4277	Inquire		8	50–75	70–80	4	26	S1, BA, B, EP
Dream Scape Villa, West End Road, Negril, 957-4495	120–180			80–120			6	BA, P, B, EP
Drumville Cove Resort, West End Road, Negril, 957-4369	45–65	64–110		30–50	40–50		11	S1, BA, P, B, EP
Foote Prints on the Sands Hotel, Negril, 957-4300/4301	Inquire		8	50	50	4	25	S1, BA, B, EP
Heartbeat Cottage, West End Rd., Negril, 957-4329	Inquire			25	25		4	EP
Hedonism II, Box 25, Negril, 957-4201	Inquire			Inquire			280	BA, P, B, AI
La Mar Guest House, West End Rd., Negril, 957-4383	Inquire			10–20	20–30		23	S1, BA, P, B, EP
Mahogany Inn, Norman Manley Boulevard, Negril, 957-4401	60–70	75–90		40–65	55–70		16	S1, BA, B, EP

Negril Accommodations (*continued*)

	WINTER			SUMMER				
Negril Beach Club, Box 7, Negril, 957-4220/1	72–110	80–110	8	34–68	42–68	4	64	S1, BA, P, B, EP
Negril Cabins, Rockland Point, 957-4350	Inquire			45				S1, BA, B, EP
Negril Gardens Hotel, Norman Manley Boulevard, Negril, 957-4408	100–110			74–80			54	BA, P, B, EP
Negril Inn, Norman Manley Boulevard, Negril, 957-4209/4370/1	140	210		140	210		46	BA, P, B, AI
Negril Palm Beach, Norman Manley Blvd., Negril, 957-4218/4418	Inquire			40–50			12	S1, BA, B, EP
Ocean Edge Resort Hotel, West End, Negril, 957-4278/4362	40–120		4	60	50		20	S1, BA, P, B, EP
Poinciana Beach Hotel & Villas, Norman Manley Boulevard, Negril, 957-4256	Inquire			40–140	44–140		41	S1, BA, B, EP
Rock Cliff Club Hotel, Negril, 957-4331	85			51–61	61–71		32	S1, BA, P, B, EP
Sundowner Hotel, Box 5, Negril, 957-4225	Inquire			45	65	6	25	S1, BA, B, P, EP
T-Water Beach Hotel, Box 11, Negril, 957-4270/1	Inquire			38–75	75	4	69	S1, BA, P, B, CP
Thrills Hotel, West End, Negril, 957-4390	65			45	44–100		20	S1, BA, P, B, EP
The Villas Negril, Box 35, Negril, 957-4250/4391/4393	Inquire			35–45	50–60			

West End as are Negril Sands, Foot Prints, and Kaiser's Cafe. Save a Dollar Supermarket and Food Fair Ltd. are at Plaza de Negril.

entertainment: Kaiser's Cafe and Alfred's On the Beach have the best live music. Try Compulseion disco which is packed with locals. T-Water, Tree House, Fish World, and Rocky Edge all have live reggae. Well known artists frequenting these places include Big Youth, Yellowman, Gregory Issacs, Echo Minot, and General Trees. Alfred's Guest House also has a great atmosphere for live entertainment.

services and sports: Most of these are located in the Plaza de Negril. Here you'll find banking facilities, a doctor, and the Tourist Board. Rite Rate Car Rental (tel. 957-4267) is at Bar-B-Barn Villas.

sports: Rhodes Hall Plantation (tel. 957-4232/4258) offers bike rentals, sport fishing, and tours. Negril Yoga Centre (tel. 957-4397) has yoga classes twice daily. Negril Scuba Centre is at the Negril Beach Club. Ray's Parasailing is near Hedonism II. Aqua Nova Water Sports is located at Negril Beach Club. Pringle Water Sports offers water skiing, parasail rides, and wind surfing. Mariner's Diving Resort (957-4348) specializes in scuba, parasailing, and water skiing. Elsewhere, bargain for water sports equipment and be sure to check its condition carefully. For riding, contact Horseman Riding Stables, tel. 957-4474.

dealing with locals: Among some really fine people, Negril has an abundance of the most obnoxious hustlers found in Jamaica. Without a single exception, everyone in the area who speaks to you without having been spoken to first is a hustler and wants something. As in other places, just don't talk to these people. Ignore them. Stone cold! They have a persistence and a level of ignorant arrogance matched in few places in the world. You can expect to be hustled many, many times per day. Don't be intimidated into buying anything; but if you're going to buy something, make sure that you bargain as if your life depended on it. And *make sure* of the quality. If these ragamuffin good-for-nothings actually stuck with the legit, they could be brilliant salesman! As it is they eke out a living selling mediocre quality herb at inflated prices and playing gigolo to naive young North American waifs who have come down to find some black banana and have no more idea of what Rastafarianism is all about than these "wolves in sheep's clothing" do. These guys are generally not dangerous except when drunk. Note that the presence of crack, however, has intensified crime. Exercise caution while in Negril. Also take care when dealing with the local hookers. These black scorpions in high heels and tight pants will take all that you have if you give them a chance. Remember that the local Jamaicans—who view this human flotsam with disdain and as a threat to their livelihood—are watching your behavior. If it's intimacy, friendship, and hospitality that you're seeking, stick with your hotel staff.

from Negril: Minibuses leave regularly for Lucea (J$3.50), MoBay (J$6), Sav-La-Mar, Mandeville, etc.

Lucea

Once a busy sugar port, it's still one of the best harbors on the north side of the island. An attractive town, it's the capital of Hanover Parish, smallest parish on the island and noted for "Lucea yam." Note the German helmet on the clock in the courthouse: it was sent by mistake. Like most such island tower clocks, this one is out of order.

sights: A short walk from town is Fort Charlotte. This classically designed 18th C. fort, named after George III's queen, stands on a peninsula overlooking the harbor it once defended. Design is simple with the remaining cannon mounted on tracks. Inside, it's overgrown with grass, and frigate birds soar overhead. It's a sharp drop to the deep blue sea below. A small crafts shop near the entrance sells bamboo, baskets, and the like. Rusea's High School, founded by the French refugee in his will, is before the fort to the right. The parish church has an attractive steeple and cemetery. **others:** Lloyd is artist-in-residence at Gallery Hofstead. Bustamante, who was Jamaica's only living national hero, was born in Blemyn, Hanover. At Bloody Bay, east of Negril, lies a nine-km stretch of totally undeveloped white sand beach. Ask the minibus driver to let you off. A beautiful view at Orange Bay.

practicalities: Edna McIntosh, a transplanted Canadian, offers basic accommodation on Church St. West Palm Hotel (tel. 956-2321) has 18 rooms and a swimming pool. There are many small restaurants in town.

GLOSSARY

ackee—fruit introduced from West Africa which is boiled and cooked together with saltfish or salt pork. National fruit of Jamaica.

aloe—medicinal plant, bitter to the taste, which originated in Southern Africa. Commonly known in Jamaica as sinkle bible.

Anancy—the Jamaican equivalent of America's Brer Rabbit. Originated with the Ghanain Asante tribe; Anancy is usually portrayed as a spider.

Arawaks—Indians who originated in the Orinoco region of South America. Supplanting earlier arrivals in the Caribbean like the Ciboneys, they were exterminated by the Spanish and by the war-like Caribs in the southern islands.

balm—system of natural medicine. Commonly practiced in Jamaica by balmists who maintain their own balmyard; treatment normally involves the use of herbs ("bush") in the form of baths and teas.

bammy—deep-fried cassava bread which originated with the Arawaks; commonly served at Jamaican roadside stands along with fried fish.

bankra—Jamaican basket; name is derived from the Twi language of Ghana (bonkara).

bauhnia—flowering plant or bush, usually with pink and lavender blossoms, indigenous to the Caribbean. A popular ornamental plant.

bauxite—ore from which aluminum is made. Jamaica at one time was the world's leading producer.

bissy—the cola nut, of African origin; a stimulant, it is used as a poison antidote, as medicine, and to make the drink of the same name.

bladderwort—a floating, insect-eating plant; commonly found on the Black River morass in Jamaica.

bulla—Jamaican traditional cake; small, flat, and round; made with flour, molasses, and soda.

cacoon—vine, found in many parts of tropical America including Jamaica. Its bean pods may extend to five feet in length.

calabash—small tree native to the Caribbean whose fruit, a gourd, has multiple uses when dried.

cassaava—a staple crop indigenous to the Americas. Bitter and sweet are the two varieties. Bitter must be grated, washed, and baked in order to remove the poisonous prussic acid. Jamaican bammy is made from the bitter variety as is casareep, a preservative which is the foundation of West Indian pepperpot stew.

cays—Arawak-originated name which refers to islets in the Caribbean.

Carib—name of Indian tribe that colonized the islands of the Caribbean, giving the region its name.

coco—Jamaican name for *tannia* and *yautia*. A staple food in the Caribbean, this tuber was originally imported from Polynesia (where it is known as taro) by the Portuguese.

coney—land mammal indigenous to the Caribbean. This small brown rodent, a favorite food of the Arawaks, has become nearly extinct owing to the mongoose and modernization.

conch—large, edible mollusk usually pounded into salads or chowders.

coratoe—also known as *karato*, maypole, and the century plant. Flowers only once in its lifetime before it dies.

doctor bird—known to the Arawaks as God bird, it was believed to be the reincarnation of a dead soul and to have magical properties

dread or dreadlocks—term connoting a Rastafarian or his hair style.

duppy—ghost or spirit of the dead which is feared throughout the Caribbean. Derives from the African religious belief that a man has two souls: one ascends to heaven while the other stays around for a while or permanently. May be harnessed for good or evil through *obeah*. Some plants and birds are also associated with duppies.

escovitch—Spanish and Portugese method of marinating seafood which has been transfused into Jamaican cuisine.

galliwasp—Jamaican lizard which is incorrectly believed to be poisonous.

ganja—Jamaican name for marijuana which was introduced into Jamaica by indentured workers from India.

guava—indigenous Caribbean fruit, extremely rich in vitamin C, which is eaten raw or used in making jelly.

guinep—small green fruit found in Jamaica and Surinam.

gungo peas—mottled green and brown peas which are a favorite Jamaican food. Commonly mixed in rice or soup, and also known as pidgeon or congo peas.

higgler—Jamaican marketeers or vendors. Traditionally female, they form the backbone of Jamaica's internal marketing system. Once the intermediary between farmer and housewife, they now board planes for Miami and Port-au-Prince and return with goods for sale.

Hussay—traditional processional festival still celebrated by Jamaica's East Indian Muslim community.

Irish Moss—Jamaican health food drink made using a seaweed extract.

jackass corn—Jamaican biscuit made from coconut and sugar.

jackfruit—yellow fleshy fruit which grows inside enormous pods extending from the trunk of the tree of the same name; seeds may be roasted or boiled and eaten.

jerk pork—famous Jamaican style of preparation originated by the Maroons and in common use throughout the island. Pimento wood gives it its special flavor. Also used to prepare chicken and fish.

jew plum—huge, greenish yellow plum which is stewed to make a Jamaican dessert. Originated in the South Pacific.

John Crow—a scavenger bird (a type of buzzard) commonly seen in Jamaica.

Jonkonnu—festivities dating from the plantation era in which bands of masqueraders, dressed with horse or cow heads or as kings, queens, or devils parade through the streets.

khus khus—grass used in making Jamaican perfume and toilet water.

Kumina (Cumina)—an ancester worship cult of Bantu origin. Very popular in Jamaica.

lignum vitae—native to tropical America. One of the most useful trees in the world. Its blue flower is the national flower of Jamaica.

love bush—orange colored parasitic vine, found on Jamaica, St. John, and other Caribbean islands. Resembles nothing so much as the contents of a can of Franco-American spaghetti.

mahoe—indigenous Caribbean tree; national flower of Jamaica.

manatee—the sea cow, mistaken by Columbus for mermaids. An endangered species, fewer than 14,000 exist in the world.

Maroons—members of runaway slave communities in the Americas. Largest group of Maroons is in Jamaica.

mento—Jamaican folk music, forerunner of calypso and reggae, now rarely performed.

myal—Caribbean white magic which became a religious cult and then faded. It included herbal medicine and the capture and control of duppies (ghosts) for positive purposes. Many of its features have been incorporated into Kumina and other revival religions.

obeah—Caribbean black magic imported from Africa. In Jamaica "bushdoctor" (herbal medicine) and "science" (based on the books of American black magician De Laurence) are practiced illegally.

ortanique—cross between a tangerine and an orange. A Jamaican fruit, its name is a combination of orange, tangerine, and unique.

otaheite apple—crimson fruit, shaped like a pear. Originated in Polynesia.

Pantomime—Jamaican annual theatrical event produced by the Little Theater Movement.

patty—Jamaican-style fast food consisting of pastry dough with spicy ground filling.

pimento—internationally known as allspice because it is said to combine the flavors of nutmeg, clove, cinnamon, and pepper. Highest quality grown in Jamaica.

rice and peas—dish made from rice cooked with beans, seasoning, and coconut milk.

sea grape—West Indian tree commonly found along beaches which produces green, inedible grapes.

sinsemilla—term used to describe the highest grade of Jamaican *ganja* (marijuana).

sorrel—originally from the Sudan, the red stems and chalices of this bushy shrub are brewed by Jamaicans to make a popular Christmas drink.

stamp and go—fried and seasoned codfish fritters found at roadside stands in Jamaica.

star apple—native of the Greater Antilles, the round fruit of this tree is always green or purple when ripe. It reveals a star-shaped pattern when sliced in the center.

tamarind—large tree producing segmented pods, brown in color and sour in taste, which are a popular Jamaican fruit.

ugli—warty and irregular citrus fruit, larger than a grapefruit. Jamaican hybrid—a cross between a tangerine and a grapefruit.

woman's tongue—Asian plant whose name comes from its long seed pods; dry when brown, they flutter and rattle in the breeze, constantly making noise.

yabba—large earthenware bowl still made in Jamaica. Of African origin, it has strong European influences in its design.

yampi—the only species of yam indigenous to Jamaica.

BOOKLIST

TRAVEL AND DESCRIPTION

Blake, Evon. *Beautiful Jamaica*. Port Antonio: Vursta Publications, 1970. Color and black-and-white photo book.

Boot, Adrian and Thomas, Michael. *Jamaica: Babylon on a Thin Wire*. New York: Schocken Books, 1976. Black-and-white photographic essay on Jamaica during the mid-70s.

Cohen, Steve. *Adventure Guide to Jamaica*. Edison, N. J. : Hunter Publishing, 1988. Color travel guide.

Fillingham, Paul. *Pilot's Guide to the Lesser Antilles*. New York: McGraw-Hill, 1979. Invaluable for pilots.

Floyd, Barry. *Jamaica: An Island Microcosm*. New York: St. Martin's Press, 1979. Concise description of island realities.

Hart, Jeremy C. and William T. Stone. *A Cruising Guide to the Caribbean and the Bahamas*. New York: Dodd, Mead and Company, 1982. Description of planning and plying for yachties. Includes nautical maps.

Morrison, Samuel E. *The Caribbean as Columbus Saw It*. Boston: Little Brown and Co.: 1964. Photographs and text by a leading American historian.

Naipaul, V. S. *The Middle Passage: The Caribbean Revisited*. New York: MacMillan, 1963. Another view of the West Indies by a Trinidad native.

Radcliffe, Virginia. *The Caribbean Heritage*. New York: Walker & Co., 1976.

Wright, Philip and Paul F. White. *Exploring Jamaica: A Guide for Motorists*. New York: W. W. Norton & Co., Inc. 1969. Outdated, but still of great value.

FLORA AND FAUNA

Adams, C. Dennis. *Flowering Plants of Jamaica*. Mona: University of the West Indies, 1972.

Avinoff, A. and N. Shonmatoff. *An Annotated List of Butterflies of Jamaica*. Pittsburgh; Carnegie Museum, 1946.

Bond, James. *Birds of the West Indies*. London: Collins, 1960 reprint.

Eyre, Alain. *The Botanic Gardens of Jamaica*. London: Andre Deutsch, 1966.

Hawkes, Alex, and Brenda Sutton. *Wildflowers of Jamaica*. Kingston: Collins-Sangster, 1974.

Kaplan, Eugene. *A Field Guide to the Coral Reefs of the Caribbean and Florida*. Princeton, N. J. : Peterson's Guides, 1984.

Lack, David. *Island Biology Illustrated by the Land Birds of Jamaica*. Berkeley and Los Angeles: University of California Press, 1976.

Romashko, Sandra. *The Shell Book of Jamaica*. Miami: Windward Publishing, 1984.

HISTORY

Ayearst, Morley. *The British West Indies*. New York: New York University Press, 1960.

Burns, Sir Alan. *History of the British West Indies*. London: George Allen and Unwin, 1954.

Hurvitz, Samuel J. and Edith F. *Jamaica: A Historical Portrait*. New York: Praeger, 1971.

Knight, Franklin W. *The Caribbean*. Oxford: Oxford University Press, 1978. Thematic, anti-imperialist view of Caribbean history.

Mannix, Daniel P. and Malcolm Cooley. *Black Cargoes*. New York: Viking Press, 1982. Details the saga of the slave trade.

Phillippo, James M. *Jamaica: Its Past and Present*. London: Dawson, 1969.

Williams, Eric. *From Columbus to Castro: The History of the Caribbean*. New York: Random House, 1983. Definitive history of the Caribbean by the late Prime Minister of Trinidad and Tobago.

POLITICS AND ECONOMICS

Barry, Tom, Beth Wood, and Deb Freusch. *The Other Side of Paradise: Foreign Control in the Caribbean*. New York: Grove Press, 1984. A brilliantly and thoughtfully written analysis of Caribbean economics.

Brown, Aggrey. *Colour, Class, and Politics in Jamaica*. New Jersey: Transaction Books, 1979.

Manley, Michael. *The Politics of Change: A Jamaican Testament*. London: Andre Deutsch, 1974.

SOCIOLOGY AND ANTHROPOLOGY

Abrahams, Roger D. *After Africa*. New Haven: Yale University Press, 1983. Fascinating accounts of slaves and slave life in the West Indies.

Barrett, Leonard. *The Sun and the Drum*. Kingston: Sangster's, 1976. Detailed account of African influence in Jamaican culture including folk medicine, witchcraft, psychic phenomena, and the language.

Brown, Aggrey. *Colour, Class, and Politics in Jamaica*. New Jersey: Transaction Books, 1979.

Clarke, Edith. *My Mother Who Fathered Me*. London: G. Allen & Unwin, 1957.

Cumper, George E. *The Social Structure of Jamaica*. Mona: University College of the West Indies, 1949.

Henriques, Fernando. *Family and Colour in Jamaica*. London: Eyre and Spottiswoode, 1953.

Kerr, Madeline. *Personality and Conflict in Jamaica*. Liverpool: Universities Press, 1952.

Kuper, Adam. *Changing Jamaica*. Kingston: Kingston Publishers, 1976. An absorbing account of social change in Jamaica.

Nettleford, Rex. *Caribbean Cultural Identity: The Case of Jamaica*. Kingston: University of Jamaica, 1979.

Nettleford, Rex. *Mirror, Mirror: Identity, Race, and Protest in Jamaica*. Kingston: Collins-Sangster, 1970. Deals with the Rastafarian movement in Jamaica and the struggle for national identity.

Norris, Katrin. *Jamaica: The Search for an Identity*. London: Oxford University Press, 1962.

Price, Richard, ed. *Maroon Societies—Rebel Slave Communities in the Americas*. Garden City: Anchor Press, 1973.

Rubin, Vera and Lambros Comitas. *Ganja in Jamaica*. The Hague, Paris: Mouton & Co., 1975. A fascinating study of the effects of marijuana usage among chronic users.

Senior, Olive. *A-Z of Jamaican Heritage*. Kingston: Heineman Educational Books, 1983. Superb, informative soft-bound encyclopedia of Jamaican history, flora, celebrations, etc.

Taylor, Frank. *Jamaica—the Welcoming Society: Myths and Reality*. Mona: University of the West Indies, 1975.

ART, ARCHITECTURE, AND ARCHAEOLOGY

Baxter, Ivy. *The Arts of an Island*. Metuchen, New Jersey: The Scarecrow Press, Inc., 1970. A survey of Jamaican arts and art history.

Buissert, David. *Historic Architecture of the Caribbean*. London: Heinemann Educational Books, 1980.

Gosner, Pamela. *Caribbean Georgian*. Washington D. C. : Three Continents Press, 1982. A beautifully illustrated guide to the "Great and Small Houses of the West Indies."

RELIGION

Barrett, Leonard. *The Rastafarians*. Boston: Beacon Press, 1977. Well-written, informative account of the Rastafarian movement including an analysis of Jamaican history and related religious movements.

Clarke, John Hendrik, ed. *Marcus Garvey and the Vision of Africa*. New York: Random House, 1974.

Cronon, E. D. *Black Moses*. Madison: University of Wisconsin Press, 1966. Detailed biography of Marcus Garvey.

Nicholas, Tracy and Bill Sparrow. *Rastafari: A Way of Life*. New York: Anchor, 1979. Rasta history and lifestyle.

Owens, Joseph. *Dread: The Rastafarians of Jamaica*. Kingston: Sangster's, 1976. An in-depth account written by a priest who taught and performed social work among the Brethren.

Smith, M. G., Roy Angier, and Rex Nettleford. *The Ras Tafari Movement in Kingston Jamaica*. Mona: Institute of Social and Economic Research.

Williams, K. M. *The Rastafarians*. London: Ward Lock Educational Books, 1981.

MUSIC

Bergman, Billy. *Hot Sauces: Latin and Caribbean Pop*. New York: Quill, 1984.

Boot, Adrian and Goldman, Vivien. *Bob Marley: Soul Rebel, Natural Mystic.* New York: St. Martin's Press, 1982. More a pictography than a biography.

Dalrymple, Henderson. *Bob Marley: Music, Myth, and the Rastas.* London: Carib-Arawak, 1976.

Davis, Stephen. *Bob Marley.* Garden City, New York: Doubleday, 1985.

Davis, Stephen. *Reggae Bloodlines, In Search of the Music and Culture of Jamaica.* New York, Anchor Press, 1977.

Davis, Stephen and Peter Simon. *Reggae International.* New York: Alfred A. Knopf, 1982. Encyclopedic coverage of reggae history, musicians, and lifestyle on a national and international level.

Green, Jonathan. *Bob Marley and the Wailers.* London: Wise Publications, 1977.

Johnson, Howard and Jim Pines. *Reggae: Deep Roots Music.* London: Proteus, 1982.

Lewin, Olive. *Brown Gal in de Ring.* London: Oxford University Press, 1952.

White, Timothy. *Catch A Fire.* New York: Holt, Rhinehart, and Winston, 1983. Dramatized account of the life of Bob Marley.

Superb discography covering Marley and everyone associated with him or the Wailers.

LANGUAGE

Beckwith, Martha. *Jamaican Proverbs.* New York: Negro Universities Press, 1970.

Cassidy, Frederick G. *Jamaican Talk: Three Hundred Years of the English Language in Jamaica.* London: Macmillan Co. Ltd., 1961. Jamaican English described.

Cassidy, Frederick G. and R. B. LePage. *Dictionary of Jamaican English*, 2nd edition. Cambridge: Cambridge University Press, 1980.

LITERATURE

Bennett, Louise, et. al. *Anancy Stories and Dialect.* Verse. Kingston: Pioneer Press, 1950.

Bennett, Louise. *Jamaica Labrish.* Kingston: Sangster's, 1966. More than 130 poems written in Jamaicatalk.

Hearne, John. *Land of the Living.* London: Faber and Faber, 1959. By the most famous of Jamaica's novelists.

Manley, Edna. *Focus: An Anthology of Contemporary Jamai-*

can Writing. Mona: University College of the West Indies, 1956.

Naipaul, V. S. *Guerrillas*. New York: Alfred A. Knopf, 1976. By one of the world's greatest living novelists—landscaped in Jamaica.

Patterson, Orlando. *The Children of Sisyphus*. Boston: Houghton Mifflin Co., 1965. Story of a prostitute attempting to rise in Jamaican society.

Sherlock, Phillip. *Anasi, the Spider Man: Jamaican Folk Tales*. New York: Macmillan, 1971.

Thewell, Michael. *The Harder They Come*. New York: Grove, 1980. Powerful and authentic portrait of Jamaica's impoverished; inspired by the film of the same name.

INDEX

Jamaica Talk: 36–39
Jerk chicken: 64
Jerk pork: 64
Jim Crow Mountains: 148
John Crow: 9
Jonkanoo: 57–58
Judgment Cliff: 153
Kapo: 43
Karstification: 3
Kenilworth: 108–109
King's House, Kgn.: 161, 170
King's House, Spanish Town: 180
Kingston: 155–183
Kirkvine Works: 203
Knibb, William: 112
Kumina: 42
Language: 36–39
Leeward Maroons: 209–211
Lignum vitae: 6
Liguanea Plain: 3
Lime Cay: 179
Linstead: 183
Little Goat Island: 185
Little Theater: 57, 168
Lluidas Vale: 185
Long Bay: 141
Lucea: 219
Mahoe: 6
Male and female relationships: 33–35
Mango hummingbird: 9
Manley, Edna: 153–161
Manley, Michael: 19–22, 26
Manley, Norman Washington: 18
Mannish water: 64
Manufacturing: 25
Marine life: 11
Maritime Museum: 179
Markets: 78, 105, 127–128
Marlborough House: 203
Marley, Robert Nesta (Bob): 20, 51–52, 53, 54, 119
Maroon Town Barracks: 210
Maroons: 15, 16
Marshall's Pen: 197
Measurements: 92

Media: 80
Mento: 50–51
Mile Gully: 203
Milk River: 185
Minard Estate: 115
Monkey Island: 139
Montego Bay: 91–110
Moore Town: 150
Morant Bay: 153
Morant Bay Lighthouse: 154
Morant Bay Rebellion: 16, 153
Morgan, Henry: 177
Mountain River Cave: 185
Music: 47–54
Myal: 41
Nanny Town: 150
National Art Gallery: 57, 159, 160
National Heroes Park: 159
National Library of Jamaica: 172
National Museum of Historical Archaeology: 179
National Theater Dance Company: 56–57
Navy Island: 143
Negril: 211–219
Nelson, Horatio: 177
New Kingston: 155, 166–167
Newcastle: 192
Nonsuch Caves: 139
Obeah: 41
Ocho Rios: 118–131
Old Harbour: 185
Oracabessa: 130
Orange Valley Estate: 115
Ortanique: 65, 195
Package tours: 72
Parade, the: 158–159
Parliament: 18
Patterson, P. J.: 22
Pellew Island: 139
People's National Party: 16, 17, 18
Pepperpot: 63
Photography: 88

Hundreds of other specialized travel guides and maps are available from Hunter Publishing. Among those that may interest you:

THE CARIBBEAN GUIDE SERIES

Each book is full color throughout and is written by an insightful local resident. Complete what to see and do information is here, with walking tours; but the guides also examine each island's geography and history, economy and politics, cultural heritage, flora and fauna, even its cuisine. *5¹/₂" x 8" paperbacks.*

ANTIGUA & BARBUDA by Brian Dyde
160 pp./$11.95

THE BAHAMAS by Gail Saunders
208 pp./$13.95

CUBA: THE OFFICIAL GUIDE by A. G. Gravette
288 pp./$17.95

CURACAO CLOSE-UP by B. Heiligers-Halabi
72 pp./$6.95

GRANADA by Norma Sinclair
136 pp./$11.95

THE ISLANDS OF BERMUDA by D. H. Raine
170 pp./$12.95

ISLANDS TO THE WINDWARD: SINT MAARTEN & SAINT-MARTIN, SAINT-BARTHELEMY, ANGUILLA, SABA, SINT EUSTA-TIUS
by Brian Dyde
128 pp./$10.95

MASQUERADE: THE VISITOR'S INTRODUCTION TO TRINIDAD & TOBAGO by Jeremy Taylor
144 pp./$12.95

NEVIS by Joyce Gordon
96 pp./$10.95

SAINT LUCIA by G. Ellis
80 pp./$6.95

ST. KITTS by Brian Dyde
128 pp./$11.95

TREASURE ISLANDS: A GUIDE TO THE BRITISH VIRGIN IS-LANDS by Larry & Reba Shepard
128 pp./$11.95

THE ADVENTURE GUIDE TO THE VIRGIN ISLANDS
by Harry S. Pariser
With spectacular beaches, panoramas and climate, these islands have a romantic history and distinct culture. The author describes in detail what there is to see and do on Saint Thomas, Saint John, Saint Croix, Tortola, Jost Van

Dyke, Virgin Gorda, and Anegada. Charts give key information about hotels and guest houses in all categories. Maps and color throughout.
5³/₈" x 8" paperback/208 pp./$13.95

THE ADVENTURE GUIDE TO JAMAICA by Steve Cohen
How to explore the real Jamaica—away from the high-rise hotels—with an emphasis on walking, canoeing, cycling, and horseback riding. The best places to stay and eat, plus sections on the black market, transportation, where to shop for authentic crafts, ganja, reggae, and everything else the visitor will want to know.
5³/₈" x 8" paperback/288 pp./color photos throughout, with fold-out color map/ $14.95

THE ADVENTURE GUIDE TO PUERTO RICO by Harry S. Pariser
The best guide to this magical island. With its abundant forest reserves, ancient Indian sites, stunning beaches, and many remains from the Spanish colonial era, Puerto Rico offers astonishing riches for the visitor. This guide tells you what to see and do in every part of the island, for the intrepid or the more relaxed visitor; where to eat and where to stay, from charming *paradores* in the countryside to the unforgettable beach resorts; how to get around; what to buy and what to avoid. The most detailed and up-to-date guide to all aspects of the island.
5³/₈" x 8" paperback/224 pp./maps and color photos throughout/$13.95

THE OTHER PUERTO RICO by Kathryn Robinson
Escaping the tourists and the crowds, this guide shows you where to find the secret beaches, unspoiled valleys, jungles and mountains of the island. Aimed at the traveller interested in outdoor adventures, each chapter explores a separate route: down the Espiritu Santo River; the Long Trails of El Yunque; beaches and birds in Guánica; tramping on Mona; scrambling through San Cristóbal; on the track of history; the heart of coffee country; Vieques by bike; and many others. Photos throughout, plus a fold-out map.
6" x 9" paperback/160 pp./$11.95

PUERTO RICO TRAVEL MAP
1:294,000 scale. Full color map shows all roads. Also includes maps of the Virgin Islands. On the reverse is an extensive text featuring practical information for the visitor.
Map measures approx. 2' x 3' unfolded/$7.95

THE CARIBBEAN TRAVEL MAP
Individual maps of Guadeloupe, Martinique, St. Lucia, St. Martin, St. Barts, and Dominica, plus an overall map of the islands. Full color cartography shows features of the terrain as well as all roads. Practical information for the visitor appears on the reverse.
Map measures approx. 2' x 3' unfolded/$7.95

HISPANIOLA TRAVEL MAP
1:816,000 scale color map of Haiti and the Dominican Republic. Practical travel information in the margins, plus individual town maps of Port-Au-Prince, Santo Domingo, and Cap Haitien.
Map measures approx. 2' x 3' unfolded/$7.95

MICHAEL'S GUIDES
Included in this series are volumes on:
ARGENTINA & CHILE
ECUADOR, COLOMBIA, & VENEZUELA

BRAZIL
BOLIVIA & PERU
Each is packed with practical detail and many maps. These pocket-sized paperbacks tell you where to stay, where to go, what to buy.
4¹/₄" x 8¹/₄" paperbacks/200 pp./$7.95 each

ALIVE GUIDES
BUENOS AIRES ALIVE
GUATEMALA ALIVE
RIO ALIVE
VENEZUELA ALIVE
VIRGIN ISLANDS ALIVE
Researched and written by Arnold & Harriet Greenberg, owners of the celebrated Complete Traveller bookstore in New York. These guides are the ultimate source for hotel, restaurant, and shopping information, with individual reviews for thousands of places—which to seek out and which to avoid. Sightseeing information as well.
5" x 7¹/₄" paperbacks/296 pp./$10.95 each

HILDEBRAND TRAVEL GUIDES
Among the titles in this series are:
MEXICO 368 pp./$10.95
JAMAICA 128 pp./$8.95
HISPANIOLA 143 pp./$9.95
The New York Times describes the series: "Striking color photographs, concise fact-packed writing, valuable practical information and outstanding cartography, including a fold-out map inside the rear cover."
4¹/₂" x 6³/₄" paperbacks

Plus

HUGO'S SPANISH PHRASEBOOK 128 pp. $3.25
Words and phrases are arranged by categories such as Hotels, Restaurant, Shopping, and Health. A special *menu guide* lists 600 dishes or methods of food preparation. An 1800-item *mini-dictionary* also included.

HUGO'S SPANISH IN 3 MONTHS $29.95
HUGO'S EL INGLÈS SIMPLIFICADO/ENGLISH FOR SPANISH SPEAKERS $29.95
These are intensive cassette-based courses in conversational speech. Each course comes in a vinyl album containing a 160-page book and four 1-hour cassette tapes designed to speed learning and to teach pronunciation. Together, the tapes and book take the absolute beginner to a good working knowledge of the language. The books are also available without the tapes at $5.95 each.

The above books, maps, and tape courses can be found at the best bookstores or you can order directly. Send your check (add $2.50 to cover postage and handling) to:

HUNTER PUBLISHING, INC.
300 RARITAN CENTER PARKWAY
EDISON NJ 08818

Write or call (201) 225 1900 for our free color catalog describing these and many other travel guides and maps to virtually every destination on earth.